SUE FISHER

GROWING UP THE WALL

HOW TO GROW FOOD IN VERTICAL PLACES, ON ROOFS AND IN SMALL SPACES

green books

First published in 2013 by
UIT / Green Books
Dartington Space, Dartington Hall,
Totnes, Devon TQ9 6EN, UK
www.greenbooks.co.uk
+44 1803 863260

Design by Jayne Jones

With the exception of the following, all photographs are by the author.
Pages 2, 27, 71, 106 (top): Burgon and Ball. Page 8: Vera Kratochvil@
PublicDomainPictures.net. Page 10: B&Q. Page 12: Dave Richards / RISC.
Pages 13, 118, 144, 148, 155: Food from the Sky. Page 18: Stephen Fry /
Aquaponics. Pages 21, 38: Paignton Zoo Environmental Park. Pages 24,
49: VertiGarden. Pages 31, 54, 58, 117: Garden Beet. Page 32: VegTrug.
Page 63: VertiFlora. Pages 67, 135: Garden Connections. Page 87:
Optigreen. Pages 78, 145, 152: Chris Coomber. Pages 109, 137: iStock.
Page 150: Jo Coomber. Page 160: Mike Coomber.

ISBN: 978 0 85784 109 4 (paperback)
ISBN: 978 0 85784 111 7 (ePub)
ISBN: 978 0 85784 127 8 (Kindle)
ISBN: 978 0 85784 110 0 (pdf)

10 9 8 7 6 5 4 3 2 1

GROWING UP THE WALL

CONTENTS

To my family: for their support and for helping with weird and wonderful projects, not to mention eating all manner of edibles without too many complaints.

Acknowledgements

Producing a book is very much a team effort: many thanks to everyone at Green Books for their expertise, support and enthusiasm, and to the many inspiring individuals, groups and companies who have helped with information and images. Of course thanks to my family; especially my Mum, who first inspired my love of plants and gardening.

INTRODUCTION

In cities and towns right around the world, gardens are, quite literally, growing up. In just a few years, it has become no longer a novelty to see tall buildings transformed from urban desert into habitat heaven, with the built environment beautified by walls or roofs clothed with a fabulous array of plants. Thanks to new technology, spaces that were previously plant-free zones can now be adapted into thriving, beneficial and beautiful growing areas, with plants in places where we never even realised there were places. This approach to growing offers something for everyone – while we may marvel at the Singapore Sky Garden or the botanical and artistic masterpiece living walls in Paris, Madrid and London by living wall pioneer Patrick Blanc, there are also many options available on a more homely scale.

So far the main trend for living walls and green roofs has been as ornamental features, along with the much-touted benefit of boosting biodiversity. But now the creation of these features is starting to meld with the massive upsurge of interest in growing edible plants. For the first time in our history, more than half the world's population live in cities. Outdoor space is more precious than ever before. Ground space for private gardens is at a premium and it goes without saying that many urban dwellers have no garden at all. Alongside this has come a quiet global revolution – a vastly increased awareness of the food we eat, where it comes from, and the environmental costs of raising crops, including the impact of 'food miles' involved in transporting our food to shops and supermarkets. Added to this is the increasing human detachment from nature, held by some to be a strong contributing factor to antisocial behaviour, vandalism and violence, and issues

The Athenaeum Hotel, Mayfair, boasts a vertical garden designed by Patrick Blanc.

such as climate change and hunger – not just the 1 billion hungry people in the world but also the global challenge of a poor diet. All these factors are encouraging countless individuals, schools, community groups and many others to look at ways of addressing these issues by growing even a small proportion of the food they eat.

In 2010 vegetable seeds outsold flowers for the first time ever in the UK as gardeners realised just how good it is to grow their own. If proof of popularity were needed, look to that apogee of garden fashion, the Chelsea Flower Show. The 2011 show was literally dominated by edibles, with the B&Q 9m (30') high 'vertical allotment' towering over other exhibits *and* winning a coveted gold medal. And Diarmuid Gavin's 'Irish Sky Garden' showed that plants could grow literally anywhere, even swinging high in the sky from a hanging 'pod'. Food-growing schemes are springing up around the world, including hundreds of community-supported agriculture (CSA) projects that involve thousands of volunteers. Many projects are aimed at making the most of tiny or previously ungardened spots, such as the Edible Bus Stop project around London's bus network and 'Incredible Edible', which began in Todmorden and is now spreading to other towns in the UK.

On an individual level, many edible plants can be grown in the smallest of spaces. For those worried about sacrificing good looks for 'edibility', fear not. Many new veg and fruit varieties are very attractive, and having plants conveniently close means you're much more likely to grab a salad for lunch, or pep up a dish with a handful of garden-fresh herbs – most of which look gorgeous too. Add edible flowers into the mix and suddenly a whole world of bright colour opens up.

Growing crops on the vertical and on roofs is a fantastic solution for space-hungry individuals, groups and communities. Whether you're

B&Q's Vertical Allotment at the 2011 Chelsea Flower Show.

an apartment-dweller with a wall, windowsill, balcony or small flat roof at your disposal, a school with nothing but a tarmac playground, or a group with just a paved courtyard in your community centre, this book is for you. Even if you have a garden already, there are benefits to be gained from growing crops in the wonderfully beneficial microclimate of a sheltered wall or fence. The rewards are many: delighting the taste buds with fresh, still sun-warmed tomatoes or strawberries, and the joy of harvesting one's own crops without any food miles whatsoever. Perhaps most of all, the sheer deep-down satisfaction of not just growing plants in hitherto impossible spots, bringing nature back into stark and bare places, but beauty with a practical purpose.

History and development

While living walls are a recent development, conceived as a combination of new technology and increased pressure on outdoor space, the concept of green roofs has actually been around for thousands of years. Traditional homes in parts of the world that experience bitterly cold winters, such as Scandinavia and Iceland, often had thick turf roofs because of their excellent insulating properties, as well as ease of maintenance. The Hanging Gardens of Babylon, built around 600 BC, was the first recorded 'green roof' garden, the great arcaded structure built with ascending terraces, roofed with bundles of reeds, layers of brick tiles and thick sheets of lead to waterproof the rooms below.

Creating growing spaces on the vertical using hanging baskets, window boxes and balcony gardens is a technique that has been in use for centuries. However, the concept of extending growing areas over the whole roof or wall, although relatively new, is edging nearer the centre of mainstream gardening. The relentless increase in population and urban growth, coupled with increased environmental awareness and the threat of climate change, has inspired a real sea change in the approach to buildings and development. Vertical and roof growing is made possible with modern materials such as highly efficient waterproofing membranes, irrigation systems and lightweight growing media, to enable the 'greening' of buildings on a grand scale. And while government policies vary around the world, of course, the change in attitudes that can be seen in many countries is immensely heartening.

To give just a few examples: in the UK, living (green) roofs and walls such as those at the O2 Arena, several shopping centres and the South Downs water treatment centre, have become major features of prominent new developments, both public and commercial, and are often a major consideration in allowing planning permission to be granted. Some states in North America, and some Canadian cities, offer tax incentives and subsidies for these features. In cities such as Copenhagen and several in Switzerland, it is now law for all roofs from flat up to a 30-degree slope to be planted. While in the main it is these large-scale commercial developments that grab the headlines, there are many inspirational small-scale features benefiting from spin-offs of the same technology. And, while commercial projects are bound to an

The roof garden at the Reading International Solidarity Centre.

exceptionally high standard in terms of quality of materials, on a domestic scale there is more scope for experimentation and DIY with simple, affordable projects using both new and recycled materials.

Community and domestic, smaller-scale projects are largely leading the way in terms of growing edible crops. These include larger food-growing initiatives that incorporate food growing on walls and roofs as part of the project, such as London-based Capital Growth, or as a self-contained roof garden such as the Queen Elizabeth Hall on London's South Bank Centre and the Reading International Solidarity Centre. In North London the 'Food from the Sky' project has created a food garden on the roof of a Budgens supermarket, with some of the produce sold in the store beneath. In September 2011, Brighton and Hove City Council published guidance notes encouraging developers to include

The 'Food from the Sky' garden on the roof of Budgens in Crouch End, North London.

food-growing space in building schemes: the first UK council to do so (see the Resources section for links to some of these examples). Slowly, surely, the future is becoming tinged with green.

Why do it?

The growing of food was once seen as a rural issue, but with a rocketing world population has come the attendant pressure on and growth of our cities, at the same time as pressure of development is shrinking our countryside. A whole range of influences has coalesced to generate today's upsurge of interest in growing our own food. But as more and more people live in cities, either with no garden space at all or where even a tiny garden is a luxury, we need to find alternative ways of growing – either by greening previously inaccessible space on walls or roofs, or by community greening of unused land, however small.

Food security and environmental impact

An awareness of the negative impact of modern living on our health and that of our whole environment is one of the main drivers behind the interest in food growing. The issue of 'food miles' has been under discussion for many years: the impact in terms of fuel consumption and pollution, of food travelling hundreds or thousands of miles from its country of origin. According to the Agricultural Organisation of the USA, the food sector accounts for 22 per cent of total greenhouse gas emissions. Diminishing oil reserves worldwide means that fuel is less available and more expensive.

But also in our post-9/11 world has come a huge understanding of the vulnerability of the food supply chain. When the aeroplanes stopped flying, yawning gaps began to appear on the supermarket shelves: no more fruit and vegetables flown from thousands of miles away. Similar scenarios occurred in 2010, when plumes of volcanic ash grounded aeroplanes in much of Europe and North America, and in the UK in 2000 when the fuel crisis caused the transport supply chain to break down. Whether the cause is act of war or terrorism, natural disaster, fuel shortage or strike, the result is the same.

Other factors are combining to slow global agricultural productivity. The Organisation for Economic Co-operation and Development (OECD) estimated in 2012 that the coming decade will see the rate slowing to 1.7 per cent, down from 2 per cent, due to a combination of factors such as higher input costs, environmental pressures and climate change. At the other end of the production chain there is an appalling level of wastage of fresh food, both by retailers and by consumers. This can be hugely reduced by having a ready supply of produce that can be harvested as required. Growing local and growing even some of our own, quite simply, makes total sense.

Cheaper, greener

The 'credit crunch' has helped people to think about reducing spending on food by growing at least some of their own produce, especially as our cooking and eating habits have changed over the years. From the simple and seasonal food of previous generations, we've become used to having an enormous range of vegetables, fruits and herbs at our disposal, available on the supermarket shelves pretty much through the year. Of course it's not possible to be self-sufficient in produce where growing areas are restricted to walls, roofs or containers, but an impressive selection of edible plants can be grown even where space is severely limited.

In terms of saving money along with growing crops that give best 'value' in terms of freshness and taste, home growers can focus on produce that commands a premium price in the shops yet which is very economical and easy to grow: rocket, watercress, mixed leaf salads and out-of-season strawberries are just a few examples. Growing premium produce is a much more effective means of offsetting the cost of the infrastructure needed to set up vertical or roof growing systems, rather than producing cheap and widely available crops such as onions, for example. Of course growing crops in the ground is always the cheapest option, but for many people who have little or no garden space, or for whom the waiting list for an allotment stretches to decades, growing in the ground is simply not an option.

Being able to grow produce organically, without using chemicals that have the potential to harm our own health and that of the wildlife and environment around us, is another big factor. The bonus of plants growing on walls, roofs and in containers is that in the main they are much easier to keep free of pests and diseases, as the environment can be controlled far more effectively than where plants are growing in the ground. Yet another benefit is being able to make the most of warm, sheltered microclimates – beneficial spots where plants particularly thrive – reducing the time between sowing or planting and harvest. Both these factors mean that crop yield can be significantly higher too. Efficient small-space organic production could help prevent agricultural intensification and the associated environmental consequences: the 2012 conference 'Food security: The value of vegetables' highlighted that the Common Agricultural Policy is driving producers towards 20 per cent organic production, which could necessitate the cultivation of millions of hectares of land outside the EU.

Benefits to the wider environment

Creating green oases comes with a whole host of environmental benefits. While the present and future effects of global warming continue to be vigorously debated, there's no denying that what we are already seeing is much greater extremes of weather all round: not just warmer but colder too, with periods of drought occurring at any time of year; stronger winds; spells of heavier rain; periods of intense heat in summer. Growing plants on buildings can help mitigate many of these extremes in the following ways:

- Insulation from summer heat and winter cold, thus reducing energy consumption, for both air conditioning and heating, and reducing human environmental impact (and household bills, of course).
- Increased life of buildings. Protecting roofs or walls from extremes of weather, including the damaging effects of ultraviolet (UV) rays in sunlight, can substantially prolong material life: studies have shown this could be as much as double their uncovered life.
- Green roofs help to absorb rainwater and reduce irrigation run-off. With flooding from heavy rain becoming more commonplace, the issue of sustainable urban drainage systems (SUDS) is becoming

much more important. Rainwater can be stored and reused to water crops. Vertical-growing systems designed to circulate water can significantly reduce rainwater run-off too.

- Boosting biodiversity. Populations of many creatures are plummeting as habitats continue to dwindle, so creating growing areas in the urban environment that can redress the balance in even a small way is immensely worthwhile. The worrying decline in bee populations is much in the headlines and beehives can, and are now starting to be, placed on roofs.

- Improved photovoltaic performance. The efficiency of photovoltaic panels decreases when the temperature of the surrounding roof rises above 25°C (77°F), yet a roof made of materials such as tiles, slates or felt can heat up to well over double that. Covering some or all of the roof with vegetation greatly reduces the temperature.

- Improved air quality. Plants are the lungs of our world, taking up carbon dioxide and giving out oxygen. In heavily trafficked urban areas, living walls and roofs help reduce pollution too.

- The 'feel-good factor'. Although hard to define, it has been suggested that gains in staff morale and well-being would far outweigh the costs of living walls and roofs on office buildings. While ornamental features are excellent, direct involvement of staff in growing (and eating) crops has even greater potential, and could even make sound business sense.

- Better public image. 'Being seen to be green' can do wonders for public perception, whether on a small or large scale.

- Community cohesion. Many urban growing projects are community based and offer an unparalleled opportunity for people to get together. For example, on Eagle Street Rooftop Farm in New York over 50 volunteers help out each week.

Not just plants

Although the focus of this particular book is on the growing of all kinds of plants, there are several other methods of food production that merit a mention in passing:

Aquaponics

Although perhaps on the edge of the scope of this book, this innovative approach to food production is worthy of mention. It combines growing plants with raising 'home-farmed' fish – a superbly common-sense method of producing food from small spaces. The system is breathtakingly simple: over a tank of water in which the fish live, plants are grown hydroponically (without soil) in trays or containers, usually filled with an inert growing medium such as clay pebbles. Water from the fish tank is pumped through the pebble bed: the plants are fertilised by the waste products produced by the fish, keeping their environment healthy and giving them a supply of clean oxygenated water. All you have to do is feed the fish, choosing a species suitable for 'farming' such as tilapia, carp, perch or even trout; as the fish grow, they produce more waste, which equals more food for the plants. When sufficiently large, of course the fish can be harvested to eat. If eating your own fish isn't to

The FishPlant unit combines two food production methods that complement each other: waste from the fish feeds the plants.

your taste, the same system can still be used with ornamental fish such as koi carp or goldfish. Aquaponics can be used on almost any scale, from the industrial to the domestic, and kits designed for the home gardener are now available.

Beekeeping

Many edible plants need to be pollinated by insects in order for the flowers to be fertilised and produce fruit, but there is a worrying decline in bee populations worldwide. If space and circumstances permit, bee-hives can be placed on green roofs and rooftop gardens; indeed urban beekeeping is becoming increasingly popular, not just on an individual level but on a larger scale too. However, it has already become so popu-lar that in late 2012 it was announced that urban bees were in danger of going hungry – a good reason to plant herbs and other nectar-producing flowers. In New York, where urban beekeeping is now legal (subject to registration), rooftop honey commands a premium price, encouraging entrepreneurs such as Chase Emmons, who harvested 135kg (300lb) of honey in 2011 from the hives at Brooklyn Grange rooftop farm and aimed to treble production over the next two years. One UK example is the Victoria Business Improvement District project in London, which has not only installed beehives but is also offering beekeeping courses to employees.

Microfarms

From chickens or bantams to small livestock, sufficient roof space may even offer the opportunity to be an urban smallholder, provided you can confine the livestock to avoid losing any growing plants. Keeping stock needs plenty of consideration, though, both from an animal welfare point of view and, of course, in an urban environment, taking into account the impact on neighbours. Do check out local regulations, by-laws and so on before going down this route.

Food for the future

Sustainable urban agriculture incorporating 'high-rise' vertical food production could provide at least part of the solution to the challenge of feeding the world's growing population. At the same time it could reduce the increasing pressure on agricultural land that is now also in demand for growing non-food crops such as fibres and biofuels.

One inspirational example in the UK can be seen at Paignton Zoo Environmental Park in Devon, with a system defined as High Density Vertical Growth (HDVG), Europe's first commercial vertical production facility. Since 2009, the VertiCrop exhibit has been growing thousands of plants – salad mixes, lettuce and microgreens – on eight-level stacking units up to 3m (10') high. As well as providing a home-grown supply of fresh food for the zoo's animals, the project also aims to demonstrate to visitors the growing, showing and eating of plants in the context of the zoo and botanical garden environment. But the benefits stretch far beyond the boundaries of the park: by improving urban food production, pressure can be taken off land – that otherwise is likely to be converted to agricultural use – hence leaving it undeveloped for the benefit of both plants and animals. HDVG, which here uses hydroponic (soil-less) growing methods (see page 36), also has great potential to link to other biological technologies such as composting of food and household waste, renewable energy generation systems which produce waste heat that can be used to warm greenhouse crops and carbon dioxide that can be used to enhance plant growth. The Paignton Zoo HDVG project is now moving further forward under a European-funded project proposal, Urban Food, which aims to establish three sustainable urban agriculture pilot projects in Belgium, France and England, exploring new technology along with promoting public awareness. The England arm of the project will form a Foundation for

The VertiCrop exhibit at Paignton Zoo Environmental Park, Devon, not only produces fresh food for the zoo's animals but also demonstrates the potential of hydroponic growing.

Research into Environmentally Sustainable Horticulture (FRESH), combining research and development of new technology with training a new generation of horticulturists in its application.

Yet on an even larger scale, the concept of 'vertical farming' in structures akin to skyscrapers, proposed by people such as Dickson Despommier, a US microbiologist and ecologist (see www.verticalfarm.com), is becoming a reality. Asian countries with overcrowded cities and a shortage of land are in the forefront of this futuristic approach to farming: South Korea, inspired by Despommier, has created both three-storey and seven-storey vertical farms in the cities of Suwon and Yongin; Japan has one in Kyoto and there are plans for a vertical farm in land damaged by earthquake and nuclear disaster near Fukushima.

In the West, the Dutch firm Plantlab is building units in Den Bosch and Amsterdam, while Sweden has plans for a seventeen-storey vertical farm. In New Orleans, the urban agriculture development company Aquaponic Modular Production Systems opened its first 'aeroponic' farm in early 2012, with 6,000 plants growing in a tower hydroponic system within a rooftop glasshouse.

Innovators are working hard and fast to create growing solutions to the world's problems. One example is the Schaduf project in Egypt, which aims to supply low-income and refugee families with micro-urban gardens so they can raise and sell their own produce. Despommier's inspiration is growing in a similar direction: he is now developing ideas for modular vertical farms that can be sent as required to places ravaged by natural or man-made disasters. Thanks to the Internet allowing ready access to inspirational design, research and technology, ideas once slated as futuristic and impractical are fast turning to reality around the world. See the Resources section for some inspiring examples.

With world population forecast by the UN to reach 9 billion by 2050 and with the chilling prospect of mass human migration if climate change renders vast areas uninhabitable or unfarmable, cities need a wealth of inspirational ideas to feed all these hungry mouths, on every scale from individual homes to vertical food-producing skyscrapers. After all, if we're falling off a cliff, in a manner of speaking, we may as well try to fly – we have nothing to lose.

PART 1

PLANNING YOUR SPACE

CHAPTER 1

Practicalities

Growing upwards on the vertical – as well as on roofs – offers incredible possibilities for the wealth of places where ground space is severely limited or downright non-existent. However, regardless of whether you have just gained a new outside area and want to start growing things to eat, or have been inspired to a new direction for an existing spot, some initial site assessment and planning is crucial to success.

While any form of small-space gardening benefits from planning to effectively squeeze the proverbial quart into a pint pot, this assumes even greater importance when growing in any sites where there are safety and structural implications. The actual growing of your crops is something well worth considering at this early stage too: the practical nitty-gritty of how to water, care for, harvest and manage plants in containers or raised on high, year on year. Gaining a clear view now of the way you will garden is likely to avoid sowing the seeds of disappointment for the future. If you're a first-time gardener, flick to the end of this chapter, where there are some useful guidelines on getting started.

Making the most of your space

This newer approach to gardening, not only upwards but on roofs too, will help you make the most of every surface in ways you may never have thought possible.

A good place to start can be a brainstorming session: standing back and taking a long, critical look at whatever space you have at your disposal. While I'm not a great advocate of gardening by committee, this can be a good approach when trying to think outside the 'traditional gardening' box. For example, someone who is a keen DIY enthusiast or salvager of discarded materials may be able to envisage many creative possibilities. If you are trying to design a school or community space, maybe even consider having a 'planning party': this suggestion is inspired by a comment from Tim Smit, founder of the Eden Project, that many of the founding groups' best ideas were produced by 'wine light'! Whether you're working alone or in a group, at this early stage it's important to jot down every idea, however wacky – bearing in mind that many of the vertical and roof-growing schemes in existence today would have been thought impossibly futuristic just a few years ago.

Almost every living environment, be it a home garden, balcony, apartment roof, school, or community space, is likely to have lots of outdoor verticals. Put together, all these sites have immense possibilities for growing a feast. Much of this is thanks to the living wall and roof technology which is a massive leap forward from the traditional approach that limited gardeners to growing climbing plants in the ground, or in containers such as hanging baskets or window boxes. However, do consider 'traditional' methods as well, maybe combining the two to get the best of both worlds and to really maximise the cropping potential from your outdoor space.

Potential growing spaces include:
- House or apartment walls. Every building has strong walls that have huge potential for growing crops, either on the walls themselves or, in the case of climbers and tall plants, grown at the base and trained upwards.
- Boundary walls and fences. Growing plants on the vertical is not only a brilliant space-saver but is often a useful green cover-up for structures that are less than attractive.
- Garden buildings. Garages, sheds, bike and garden stores have lots of growing potential not just on their sides but roofs too, so long as the structure is sufficiently strong or can be made so.
- Out-of-sight roofs. Home extensions, garages and other buildings may have roofs with planting possibilities (for more on roof practicalities see page 98).

Assessing your site

The practicalities, along with the pros and cons, of living walls and green roofs are covered in more detail in Chapters 2 and 3. The following is a brief overview of the main points relating to both.

This Hampton Court Flower Show garden by Burgon and Ball demonstrates just how much food can be produced from a small space using new growing methods.

Planning

Urban planners are broadly very much in favour of 'green' features; indeed with new-build applications or building conversions, an eco-friendly green roof, for example, may well tip the balance in terms of whether the planning authority takes a favourable view or not. While small-scale features, particularly retrofitted ones, are unlikely to need planning consent, when in doubt do check with just a quick phone call or email to the planning department of your local council.

Landlord or owner consent

If you do not actually own a building, or the boundary wall or fence that you're eyeing with interest, it is essential to get permission from the owner before starting to construct anything like a living wall or roof that will form a major feature. If you own your home, the title deeds should clarify the ownership of the boundaries. However, even when you own the site, if your neighbour is likely to be affected in any way, do have an informal word with him or her first for the sake of peaceful relations – it could avoid an enormous amount of hassle and years of bad feeling. This is vital if you want to create a feature that would be overlooking someone else's home or outdoor space, such as turning a flat roof into a green roof garden or building a high deck to make a garden platform. The old saying 'good fences make good neighbours' could be adapted in this case to 'a bit of privacy makes for peaceful relations'.

Safety

Once you leave ground level in any way and particularly if going on to a roof, safety must be absolutely and totally paramount. A green roof that will be walked on, or a roof garden, simply must have a secure barrier around the edge. If your mode of access to a wall-growing or roof-growing space is via a set of steps or a ladder, the base and top must have secure spots on which to rest, and ideally be secured there too – even if just with removable wire loops, or hooks. If there are children of any age around, bear in mind that they are likely to find ladders irre-sistible to climb so safety is doubly important. Be aware that visiting children need even more supervision as they won't be as familiar with the site and any potential dangers as resident children are. The ideal is a permanent stairway, with non-slip treads and a handrail, and which can be fitted with a safety gate if there are very young children around.

Structural stability and waterproofing

When constructing a green roof or attaching containers of any sort to a wall, there must be no danger of this causing any damage whatsoever, either by the weight causing physical damage, by water seepage down through a roof, or by the method of attachment piercing a protective coating such as render or plaster. Always bear in mind that plants + growing medium + water can add up to a considerable weight. When growing plants on roofs, it may be necessary to install a root barrier membrane as well as a waterproofing layer, to prevent roots questing down and working their way into the roof itself.

Ease of access

This may be stating the blindingly obvious, but only grow crop plants if you can actually access the area safely to maintain, water and harvest them. If a site can be accessed, but perhaps *not* quickly or easily, choose crops that aren't so demanding of regular care and attention – garlic, carrots and herbs rather than tomatoes and beans, for example.

Water

A regular supply of water is absolutely essential, as plants on a roof or a sunny wall or fence will dry out rapidly. The ideal, from an eco-friendly and a cost point of view, is rainwater. This can be stored in a variety of ways, from traditional water butts to built-in underground storage chambers (see pages 38-41). Some form of access to mains water is advisable as a backup, though, for times when stored supplies run dry. However, if lack of water is likely to be an issue, there are many herbs and edible flowers that are tolerant of drier conditions.

Cost

There are various ways of using containers and putting them together to make living wall growing solutions that can be created inexpensively by various DIY methods, and large-scale manufactured wall units and green roofs do not come cheap. In the case of green roofs, unless you are an ardent and capable DIY enthusiast, the larger roofs are best installed by professionals, which can be particularly costly. However, small-scale green roofs on buildings such as sheds, car ports, bicycle shelters, even chicken and animal runs, lend themselves much more readily to a DIY approach and hence are much cheaper to construct (see page 96).

Planning your planting

Every site will have its pros and cons for planting, mostly related to mini-microclimates that are subject to sun or shade, wind or drought, so the advantage of planning is to make the very most of what you have. A good place to start your planning is with old-fashioned pencil and paper to make a rough sketch of your site. Techies are likely to prefer the computer-aided approach, while a good way to plan that falls between these two methods is to photograph your space, print an enlargement and use an overlay of tracing paper for making notes.

Sun

Most important, because you simply can't change this one! The vast majority of cropping plants need at least several hours of sun a day in order to thrive and produce a worthwhile crop. Note down where the sun shines, for roughly how long and at what time of day – bearing in mind that this will vary hugely at different times of year, as the sun is highest in the sky during summer. A compass to determine direction is a useful aid but remember that small spaces will be strongly influenced by factors such as nearby buildings, overhanging trees and the like.

A site that gets sun for at least half the day is essential for most plants to crop well, fruit in particular. Identifying and making the most of sheltered micro-climates will pay dividends in both crop quantity and quality.

Wind

Become familiar with where the wind blows: one side of a building may be snugly sheltered from the prevailing breeze, but go round a corner or through a gate and it could change to a howling gale. As with sunshine, wind varies with the seasons – a gentle, pleasant breeze in summer can become an Arctic blast in winter. Buildings, particularly tall ones, funnel the wind and a narrow street may well create a real 'wind tunnel' effect. Roofs are an especially harsh environment for plants in terms of exposure to wind. In many situations, however, you may be able to protect your growing environment by putting up screening of some type to filter or deflect the wind from your crops.

Wind is far more of an issue at roof level than on the ground.

Indoor impacts

Don't forget to consider any knock-on effect that your plans may have on your living space too; for example, a plant-covered pergola outside may seem like a great idea when summer sun creates a soft dappled shade, but could turn a room into a cold, shady cave in winter. However, your view from inside out can be greatly enhanced by growing plants on walls and fences that have previously been bleak and bare, so consider this aspect when choosing a location. One particular advantage of shallow wall containers such as troughs, hanging bags, window boxes and ready-made 'living wall units' (see page 55) is that these occupy very little depth, making it possible to plant space that is extremely restricted width-ways, such as along pathways or entrances.

Growing inside

Although food crops are usually thought of as almost exclusively outside, containers and wall units that are neat and non-drip are perfect for growing edible plants inside as well. Large plastic bottles are ideal for this purpose: they can be adapted into containers and used individually – the 5-litre (8¾ pint) size is good to use alone – or 2-litre (3½-pint) ones can be combined in a home-made frame (see page 77). There are ready-made units for indoor use too. Plenty of light is the one essential requirement; this could be in a porch, conservatory, a kitchen with large windows or roof lights, or even in a living room. However, now that low-energy LED lights are widely available, growing indoors with supp-lementary lighting is a feasible proposition even on a domestic scale. The fact that businesses such as Podponics in the USA (see Resources section) are growing a wealth of crops inside old shipping containers brings home the realisation that food really can be grown anywhere.

Take photographs

Lastly, do take plenty of photographs to begin with and as you progress: as your project develops, it's a real morale-booster to look back on what you have achieved.

Beware the pollution trap

Plants are the lungs of our world and could be described as 'clean air devices', taking up carbon dioxide and giving out oxygen. Although this is a big plus in most cases, when growing edible plants it is best to avoid 'street canyons' – heavily trafficked urban roads that are edged on both sides with tall buildings. Until recently, it had been thought that green wall plants only reduced pollution levels by around one or two per cent, but research carried out by the University of Birmingham and Lancaster University, published in 2012, estimates this figure as in excess of ten per cent. Plants also trap particulate matter – which again is great for improving air quality, but not great for crops heading for the table.

Growing practicalities

The smaller the space and the more restricted the growing area, the more it will pay to give plenty of attention to the basics, particularly on walls and roofs which can be more challenging places for plants to grow. Selecting the best compost or growing medium, regular watering and feeding, will all make an enormous difference to plant performance and hence the crops produced.

Choosing the right growing medium

A good foundation in which to grow is absolutely essential if fruit and vegetable plants are to perform well and produce a decent harvest. In traditional container growing this would mean simply buying a good-quality potting compost, and this is the case for small living wall and roof setups. However, for larger-scale installations weight is the overriding factor for obvious reasons: using soil or soil-based compost would result in ultra-heavy containers or wall units that would be hard if not impossible to attach securely, or roofs that would need to be substantially strengthened.

In addition to being lightweight, the medium in which plants are grown must also be good at retaining water and nutrients for vegetables and fruit, which mostly tend to be hungry and thirsty plants. The situation is different for a good proportion of herbs and edible flowers, many of which are tolerant of dry soils and a shallow growing medium. You can of course decide to do without soil altogether if you go for a soil-less or hydroponic growing system (see page 36).

Large green roofs have their own particular requirements, and commercial growing media or substrates have been developed specifically for them (see page 97).

Compost

There is an old gardening saying that 'the answer lies in the soil', and this is never truer than when growing plants where their rooting area is restricted. In order for plants to perform well, they simply need the best you can give. Always buy good-quality potting compost (cheaper in bulk if you need a lot), but never try to skimp and use alternatives. I'm often asked about using garden soil or used potting compost – the answer is a firm 'no' in both cases. Soil dug out of the garden or from the ground elsewhere is not only extremely heavy, but the physical structure just isn't suited to growing in a very small space where roots need a carefully balanced structure with enough air spaces as well as a good nutritional balance. Potting compost that has been previously used is not only exhausted of nutrients but is likely to have degraded structurally too, and is likely to harbour pests, disease spores or weed seeds into the bargain.

Weight is usually the most important consideration with living walls, hanging or raised containers and containers on roofs, so avoid heavy soil (loam)-based compost such as the John Innes types and go for soil-less compost: this is the most widely available type and is usually labelled 'multipurpose'. For environmental reasons I always prefer those based on recycled material rather than peat, although be sure to buy a good-quality brand as cheaper, inferior composts are sadly plentiful. In particular, be aware of those containing an abnormally high level of insufficiently rotted recycled green waste: this is likely to smell strongly when the bag is first opened and, because the woody material is too fresh, will draw nitrogen from the compost as it completes its breakdown process. Wherever weight is not an issue, and particularly if you want to grow long-lived crops ('long' as in more than a year, such as strawberries or berry fruits), it's always worth using at least a proportion of soil-based compost. This performs better in the longer term, the loam providing more of a buffer against drought and being better at holding on to nutrients.

If you're new to gardening, be aware that when going to a garden centre or store to buy compost you are likely to be faced with a bewildering range of different products in large and brightly coloured bags. Avoid anything labelled 'soil conditioner', 'mulch' or 'composted manure', all of which are designed for use in garden borders, not containers. 'Potting compost' is what you need for any form of container or restricted-space growing.

Two downsides of compost – and this will depend on the location of your growing site – is that it is (a) heavy and (b) bulky. Not a problem if you can unload a few bags from your car boot, or can receive a delivery, but potentially a large stumbling block if it needs to be carted up several flights of stairs or up on to a roof. If only a small amount is needed, buy blocks of dry, compacted coir compost, which swell up to a satisfying bulk when water is added. It's more expensive than normal compost but the cost is balanced out by convenience.

However, there is another option to consider: growing without any soil or compost whatsoever.

Hydroponics: growing without soil

Plant roots must have water, nutrients and oxygen, but they can be grown perfectly well in a solution of nutrients dissolved in water, without any soil at all. This method of culture is called hydroponics and is becoming increasingly popular for raising crops, on every scale from small domestic setups to large commercial growing units. Being lightweight and space-saving, this system is often used for large-scale vertical-growing systems, including living walls and on green roofs with

plants growing in modular units. Plants can either be grown:
- In an inert medium (such as clay granules, sand, perlite or vermiculite: the latter two are expanded volcanic aggregates).
- In a system that supports the plant but without any medium at all.

Because still water rapidly becomes airless and stagnates, a hydroponic system recirculates the solution – usually by means of an electrically powered pump – in order to maintain a healthy growing environment for the roots. However, of the two approaches, consider the advantage of using a growing medium: the roots have greater protection against drying out if the pump or nutrient solution supply fails for any reason.

In addition to not needing soil, hydroponic growing offers several advantages over raising plants in soil or potting compost:
- Plants form smaller, more fibrous root systems, hence grow more efficiently and produce higher yields.
- Water and nutrients are reused within the system, so there is little or no waste, or drainage issues, and less water is required than with traditional growing methods.
- There are fewer pests and diseases, which would otherwise be harboured in the soil. Hence there is no need to bother about growing different crops in the same spot over subsequent years (a process known as crop rotation).
- 'Clean' growing systems are much more appealing to use indoors or where space is very limited and has to be kept neat and tidy.
- Automated systems are low maintenance, only needing attention every couple of days.

The disadvantages are:
- Such systems are likely to cost more initially.
- Automated systems require access to electricity.

Growing hydroponically avoids having to lug compost into awkward sites. Plants develop excellent root systems and produce good harvests too.

- Most systems are obviously more complex than simply planting crops in any form of container and watering by hand. However, ready-made kits for the home gardener are widely available and this system of growing is becoming increasingly popular for crop plants on walls and roofs.

Many large-scale vegetable or fruit production units now grow hydro-ponically (see page 20 for details of several large-scale operations that use hydroponic growing), and of course there is huge potential for developments in the future.

Water storage, watering and irrigation

All edible crops will require water in varying amounts, so it is vital to build this into your plans right at the beginning. While access to the mains is advantageous as it provides a reliable and convenient supply, there are several good reasons to look at alternatives. There are the ecological implications of ever-increasing demands on national water resources; the increasing spectre of hosepipe bans in times of drought;

plus the fact that most mains water supplies are metered these days so you pay for what you use.

Harvesting rainwater saves using mains supplies, which are increasingly under pressure: for much of the year water is readily available, costs nothing apart from the mode of collecting, and is better for your plants because the pH (level of acidity/alkalinity) is balanced. Rainwater is also free from chlorine, which is usually added to tap water. Another option to consider is household waste water, generally referred to as grey water (see page 41).

Consider, too, whether you want to do your watering by hand (and bear in mind this could be up to twice a day in hot, breezy weather when levels of evaporation are extremely high) or whether to go for some type of irrigation system – either a low-tech and low-cost or no-cost DIY one or a manufactured one (see page 42).

Rainwater harvesting

Even a small roof collects plenty of rainwater, so do consider the different ways of tapping into this free and eco-friendly supply. However, if your water storage will be sited anywhere apart from on the ground, whatever form of butt or tank you buy you will need to consider its weight. This may sound obvious, but water is heavy; just think how much your arms ache after carting around buckets and cans. One litre (1¾ pints) weighs approximately one kilogram (2lb 3oz), so bear this in mind if siting a butt, tank or similar container on a roof or balcony.

Simplest and cheapest is a water butt, connected to a downpipe using a rainwater diverter (when the butt is full, the diverter closes to avoid overflowing and sends water back down the drainage pipe). If you have only one downpipe, it is straightforward to link several butts together so one overspills into the next. Basic water butts are often available at discount prices from water companies and sometimes from local councils: there's a huge range on the market in different sizes, shapes, styles and of course price tags. If you want one that looks like a Roman column, a Greek urn, or with a built-in watering jug, you can have it – at a price. It is worth weighing up the cost of water saved against outlay, as the snazziest designs cost several hundred pounds. Another option is a 'pop-up' design, a brilliant and useful idea as they can be 'collapsed' and easily stored at cooler or wetter times of year when water supplies aren't in great demand.

Important points to look for when choosing rainwater storage are cost, capacity, physical footprint and carbon footprint. Of course the larger the better in terms of quantity of water stored, though space is often the limiting factor. Square butts, though less common, make much better use of space than round ones, especially if several are linked together. Also worth looking at is how much recycled plastic has been used in the manufacture. But any large, clean container can be used to gather and store rainwater, so long as it didn't contain anything toxic in a past life. Keep an eye out at your local tip, car boot sale or agricultural auction: those that look less than attractive, such as bright blue food barrels, can be tucked behind trellis screens clothed with climbing beans or berry fruits.

It's a good idea to cover any containers used to gather rainwater. It avoids accidents to pets, children, birds and other wildlife; prevents sunlight encouraging lots of algal growth that turns the water green; stops mosquitoes and midges using it as a breeding ground; and keeps out leaves that would otherwise rot down and contaminate the water. Do also put some sort of filter over the inlet to your storage container, to prevent leaves and other debris getting in. While you can buy special

Rainwater storage ideas

Think outside the box (or in this case, butt) when saving and storing water. Traditional water butts can gobble up a lot of precious outdoor space and, while there are slimline, space-saving, wall-mounted models, they're a lot dearer than basic ones. Go underground with rainwater storage tanks that are designed to go under patios and decks: some are built strong enough to even withstand vehicle traffic. Needless to say, tailor-made ones as robust as this are costly, but where weight is less of an issue – such as under a deck used for sitting out – it's perfectly feasible to do a low-priced DIY job. One good example I have seen used is a large plastic tank that was surplus to the local plumber's requirements, dug into a bank with a wooden deck over the top. A cheap submersible pond pump was used to draw out the water into a garden hosepipe as required.

Using a small pump and a hose is a simple way to avoid the slow and arm-aching process of transporting water from tank or butt via watering cans or buckets to lots of wall units or containers. While many pumps need to be powered by electricity, there are now some excellent small solar-powered models on the market.

filters to fit to downpipes, I find the leg from old nylon tights or stockings, tied or gaffer-taped over the inflow, does a reasonable job.

Reusing household water

Although some 'grey water' can be used for ornamental plants (once cooled, of course), the water used for laundry, bathing and showering can transmit bacteria and disease, so for this reason is not recommended for use on edible crops. Water from preparing vegetables is fine to use, as is that from washing dishes so long as it's not really greasy or dirty, but don't use waste water from dishwashing machines as the strong detergents are harmful to plants. Use water straight away, as stored washing-up water very soon starts to become septic and smelly. If you use the same can or bucket to apply grey water on a regular basis, do give it a frequent, thorough clean to avoid a build-up of bacteria.

Watering or irrigation systems

Some ready-made 'living wall units' incorporate built-in irrigation and so all that is required is to set up a supply of water to the inlet on the unit (see page 60). Otherwise, there are plenty of watering systems for the ordinary gardener, from inexpensive and low-tech starter kits to professional-level irrigation. I recommend avoiding the use of sprinklers, which are wasteful and lose a lot of water by evaporation, and opt for a system that delivers water directly to the plants' roots, either via porous pipe or by individual drippers. Porous pipe, made from recycled car tyres, is sometimes called 'leaky hose' as the water percolates out along its entire length. A drip system consists of short sections of narrow tubing that lead off a larger, main pipe, and this type needs a little more planning in the setup to ensure the drippers are in the right places for various crop plants (for example, courgette plants will need to be spaced much further apart than lettuce).

Going fully or partly automatic has several big advantages:
- Ease of maintenance: add a timer to your system, and you don't even have to be there to turn on the tap.
- Automation makes it easier to water when it's better for your plants rather than you (see box on page 45).
- Irrigation systems deliver a steady trickle of water right to the plants' roots, rather than the potentially damaging gush from a hose.
- Watering systems aren't subject to hosepipe bans in times of drought.

However, you need to remember that systems do need checking from time to time. Nozzles get blocked, pipes split, timers run out of battery, water butts run dry. There have been some high-profile living walls that have died in a spectacular, newsworthy fashion, simply because the irrigation failed and *no one noticed* until it was too late. A quick, regular check can avoid things ending in tears: just by sticking a finger in the soil or growing medium to make sure it is moist, or looking closely at the plants to see if they are drooping.

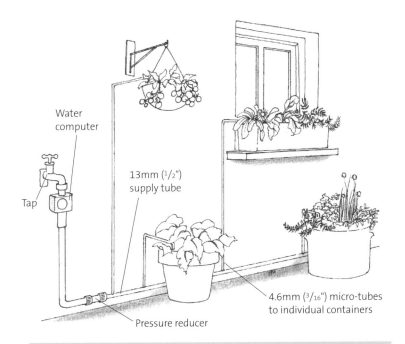

Water computer

13mm (¹/₂") supply tube

Tap

4.6mm (³/₁₆") micro-tubes to individual containers

Pressure reducer

Layout of an irrigation system.

Small-scale and low-tech watering devices

If you only have one or two wall units or a few containers to care for, a watering system may be more than you need. Turn to these simple approaches to avoid the tyranny of having to water regularly:

● Plastic bottles can be turned into individual watering devices. For accurate watering, fit each one with bottle-top watering spikes in place of the screw top. (Don't confuse this type with bottle-top waterers that turn a bottle into a mini watering can.)

● 'Water slices' are made of a sponge-like material that is soaked in water for several hours then placed in a container where it slowly releases the water into the compost.

● Use containers that are 'self-watering' (with a built-in reservoir).

● Separate 'self-watering' reservoirs can be bought and retrofitted to ordinary containers.

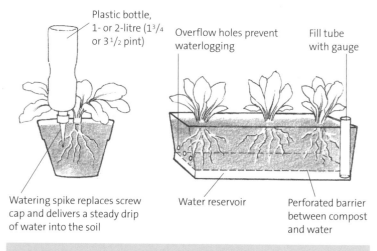

Plastic bottle, 1- or 2-litre ($1^3/_4$ or $3^1/_2$ pint)

Overflow holes prevent waterlogging

Fill tube with gauge

Watering spike replaces screw cap and delivers a steady drip of water into the soil

Water reservoir

Perforated barrier between compost and water

Left: bottle-top waterer. Right: 'self-watering' container.

Watering and feeding tips

Plants in containers of any sort, or on living walls, are rather like pets – they depend on you for everything, for nutrients (in the form of fertiliser) as well as water. The key points to follow for success are:

- Either mix a controlled-release fertiliser into the compost when planting, which will feed your crops for several months, or use a liquid feed on a weekly basis during the growing season.
- Choose a fertiliser with a nutrient balance to suit the plants you are growing. For example, fruit-producing plants such as tomatoes need a fertiliser high in potassium to boost crop production, whereas leafy vegetables need more nitrogen. There's an extensive range of fertilisers available to suit these different crops.
- Watering requirements vary depending on position: part-shaded plants use far less water than those in the sun. Similarly, plants exposed to wind dry out much faster than those in sheltered sites. In wind *and* sun they dry the fastest!
- Timing is important: avoid watering while plants are in direct sunlight, because not only is more water lost by evaporation but, also, water droplets act like little magnifying glasses and can cause unsightly scorch marks on foliage, flowers and fruit. The best time to water is the evening, so the compost and plants have the whole night to absorb water. The next best time is early morning.
- Try not to let compost dry out completely. If this does happen, it may be necessary to water sparingly but repeatedly until thoroughly moistened. If possible, take down the container and submerge it in water for an hour or so to thoroughly re-wet it.
- Mulch the surface of the soil to reduce the amount of water lost by evaporation. Various materials can be used, depending on how good it needs to look. Bark chips, cocoa shell, gravel or stone chippings are attractive.

Vertical gardening basics

When growing edible plants on the vertical or in very small spaces, it's worth checking out the basics regardless of whether you are a first-time gardener or a more experienced one who is having a try at an alternative way of gardening. While there's not enough space in this book to cover many basics of gardening in detail, here are my top tips when making your first forays into growing edibles in this way.

Start small

If you've had little or no experience of growing plants for food, feel your way in gently with, say, one or two 'living wall units' or a few containers, rather than going for a large ambitious setup straight away. It can take a while to get used to the 'little and often' approach to care that most crop plants need, and to fit it into your routine. Make sure your gardening is a pleasure, not a chore.

Start with simple crops

Plants are not equal in their demands and growing habits: distinguish between easy or difficult, fast or slow, pest- and disease-prone or tough cookie, and you'll be off to a flying start.

Quick

My favourite starter crops are salads, in many forms. Leafy crops are brilliant to home-grow and harvest fresh as they deteriorate so fast on the shop shelves. Mixed salad leaves come in many variety blends and flavours to suit different tastes, and different mixes can be sown at different times of year. In warm weather you could be harvesting your first leaves just a few weeks after sowing. Loose-leaf lettuce, baby spinach, radishes, beetroot to harvest as 'baby beet', rocket and oriental leaves such as mizuna are all speedy customers.

Slower and easy

Soft fruit, most herbs and many edible flowers fall into the 'plant; sit back and wait' category. When it comes to fruit, strawberries are the quickest fruit to grow, especially if you buy 'misted tip' plants to put in during autumn (see page 142). Ready-grown vegetable plants (see below) such as tomatoes, peppers, courgettes, pumpkins and beans, planted out in early summer, will produce a good crop within several months.

Buy time

The quickest approach is to simply buy young vegetable plants that can be planted and get growing straight away. You'll find a reasonable range at garden centres, nurseries and farmers' markets, but for the widest choice of varieties, order online from specialist suppliers – just make sure plants won't turn up when you're away for a couple of days, as they'll need unpacking immediately. If you're unsure what to grow, many suppliers offer different collections to save you having to order individual varieties. Just make sure you have the timing right for those that can't take the frost (see below). There's more information on choosing your plants on pages 109-114.

Take care with tender plants

Certain vegetables are frost tender, which means plants mustn't go outside until the last frosts have passed; at worst they could die and at best they may be severely checked and end up weeks late. Of course the 'last frost' date varies by several weeks according to where you live, from mid-spring to early summer; when in doubt, ask around any gardening friends or talk to staff at your local nursery or garden centre. This is another example of where vertical gardening scores yet again: a sunny wall or fence creates a beneficial mini-microclimate that is warmer than unsheltered parts of the garden and hence more favourable for tender plants. Here too it is easier to rig up temporary shelter for tender plants, which is handy when a late frost is forecast.

The easiest way to grow tender crops such as tomatoes, runner and French beans, cucumbers, courgettes, sweetcorn, peppers and aubergines is simply to buy young plants once the weather has warmed up. To grow them from seed, sow indoors from early to mid-spring and grow on a sunny windowsill in a heated room. If you buy plants that have been growing in greenhouses or polythene tunnels – very likely if buying by post or online – they will need to be acclimatised gradually to the outside world over a couple of weeks, a process known as 'hardening off', before they finally go outdoors.

Ring the changes

'Crop rotation' at its simplest means swapping your crops around so they aren't grown in the same spot, in the same soil, for two or three years on the trot. So if you have a raised bed or a green roof, don't keep growing tomatoes, for example, in the same spot. The reason for this is that certain plants that are prone to pests and diseases are likely to sicken and even die if not given a fresh start. Where you're growing fruit or vegetable crops in smaller containers, it's a good idea to have a complete clear-out every year or two by emptying out the soil and giving the container a good wash with hot water and then using fresh compost for new plants.

CHAPTER 2

Edible living walls

While good old window boxes and hanging baskets have been popular for balcony and courtyard planting for centuries, now container gardening meets grow-your-own with a truly twenty-first-century twist, as diminishing ground space encourages the growing trend for vertical edibles. Well-planted walls, fences

and other verticals can look fabulous just with edibles: a combination of beautifully shaped and coloured leaves, handsome herbs and a scattering of jewel-like edible flowers. There's a wealth of opportunities to be creative, with both the containers themselves and the planting.

The size and sturdiness of your wall, fence or any other vertical feature is the only limit to the number of containers that it can hold. A surface can be packed with some of the more 'traditional' ones mentioned later in this chapter, or take the idea further and cover the whole area with plants. There are now many commercially available products for this purpose, and such ready-made products can be tempting, especially in terms of looks and convenience. You could also use these for inspiration to make your own: troughs on frameworks, for example, perhaps combined with trellis so plants can grow up as well as out or down; or troughs in diminishing sizes, stacked up to create plantings that are both beautiful and edible.

Inevitably, of course, commercial designs come with a price – quite a high one in some cases. In these days of tight budgets and an increased awareness of environmental issues, budding 'vertical gardeners' will be relieved to know that there are plenty of ingenious recycled and home-made options. There's a range of my favourites in this chapter (see pages 75-78), but the great thing about plants is that anything that can hold compost and have drainage holes made in it can be turned into a container. Keep this thought in the back of your mind all the time and a whole world of planting possibilities starts to open up.

Vertical growing to suit your site

The size and structure of your garden or potential growing area is very likely to strongly influence your choice of containers or growing method.

These can be broadly divided into the following categories.

- Wall-mounted – includes the good old hanging basket, mangers, half-baskets (see page 66) and suspended growing bags (page 72), now joined by lots of ready-made innovations, mainly in the form of modular fabric planters (page 58) and modular panels, either with planting pockets or flat (pages 59 and 60). Window boxes and troughs (page 68) can also be used in this way.

- Ground-based but vertical structures attached to a wall, fence or framework, either just for stability or to take some of the weight. Examples include the Modu-wall, the Polanter, Easiwall troughs on a framework (page 62), and the home-made trellis-and-bottle wall (page 77).

- Pots or tubs with a small footprint, which may go at the base of a wall (or balcony edge) for a climber to grow up the wall. Climbing plants are discussed on page 79.

Note that containers with a larger footprint, so suitable for larger flat areas such as a roof garden, are covered in Chapter 4. These may include a vertical structure built up from the container (for example, 'ladder allotments', page 104).

Pros and cons of high-rise container gardening

Before flipping ahead to be inspired by all the different ways of growing, just take a few minutes to read through the benefits, along with the odd disadvantage to be aware of, when taking your crops into the vertical dimension. While making the very most of available space is the overwhelming and obvious advantage to growing on the vertical, there are a number of other factors that all contribute to make this an even more appealing way to grow your own food.

Pros

Making the most of microclimates. Any wall that gets a reasonable amount of sun creates a noticeable 'storage-heater' effect that will help you grow better crops and achieve harvests that start earlier in the season and carry on for longer. To see why, try this: several hours after the sun has gone down following a warm day, touch the wall and feel the heat continuing to radiate out. Yet move your hand less than half a metre or so away and the temperature plummets. This alone should be enough to convince anyone to clothe their walls with plants and reap the benefits of improved growth! The same storage-heater effect continues to operate in winter, creating a microclimate several degrees warmer than elsewhere that protects plants from the worst extremes of winter frost. The benefits of a protected site can be further developed with the use of crop protection fabrics or plant shelters (see opposite).

Easy access. The majority of cropping plants need attention little and often, even if it's just to pull off the odd dead leaf or harvest the most succulent and ripest fruit. And, from a physical point of view, a lot of bending and stooping isn't ideal at any age, but it's a really bad idea for anyone with any muscular, back or mobility problems. There are other advantages (not health related) at the other end of the age spectrum with primary-age children in schools, where growing crops high up has distinct advantages. Children have a great tendency to become mud magnets, and growing plants off the ground avoids too much contact with the soil: useful if running a lunchtime gardening club, for example, where there just isn't time to get a group changed into wellies and overalls, or if doing some plant study as part of a lesson. The other benefit is less obvious: the excitement of being outside, of discovering the first strawberries or a visiting ladybird, makes all but the most sensible children forget where to put their feet!

Healthy growth. Trained or planted above the ground, there is more space for plants to grow and spread and for more sunlight to reach the leaves, hence plants thrive better and grow more strongly. This is aided by plenty of air circulation around the flowers, fruit and foliage helping to keep fungal diseases at bay, because the spores of most diseases absolutely flourish in damp, humid, 'stagnant' air. It's useful to remember that fungal diseases cannot be cured – only prevented – and this is done primarily by creating good growing conditions.

Protection from pests. Many of these, particularly those prime gardeners' enemies, slugs and snails, live on and around the garden floor – in dead leaves, plant debris, under leaves, stones and stumps. They are much less likely to venture up into the airy heights of raised containers (although not unheard of, so don't be complacent – I have caught snails up at first-floor level). However, when there is only a limited zone of entry (such as up the stem or along the base of the wall or fence) it is much easier to establish some form of protection and also to stick to organic methods of pest control, which is so much better for the garden environment and its wildlife. Many pests, such as caterpillars and flea beetles, can be kept at bay by covering the crop with fine netting or horticultural fleece; the same applies when it comes to keeping birds away from succulent ripe fruit. And if you grow carrots more than (adult) waist height off the ground, you'll have no trouble with carrot root fly, which simply doesn't fly that high!

Protected cropping. While a wall or fence creates a beneficial microclimate in its own right, adding an extra layer of protection enables the gardener to extend the growing period even further, to harvest crops much earlier and later in the season. Growing plants on the vertical gives lots of potential to rig up a variety of crop covers made out of fleece or polythene; to grow plants in an inexpensive ready-made polythene

Gardening off the ground (here in modular fabric planters) keeps crops clean and out of reach of most garden pests too.

plant house; or spend a bit more and invest in a lean-to greenhouse. Protected cropping is especially worthy of consideration if you live in a cold, windy or rainy region. As well as creating a warmer microclimate in spring, autumn or winter, if you have a south-facing and sun-baked site, plants may also benefit from protection from the sun in high summer, which can be done using horticultural shade netting.

Cons

Water. Plants in containers are very much like pets – they rely on you for almost everything they need, particularly a steady supply of water in order to survive and thrive, as well as plenty of food (see page 45). Rain is very, very rarely enough when gardening vertically, due to the 'double whammy' of conditions: overhanging roof eaves keep off pretty much all the rain that falls, while a warm sunny microclimate speeds up water loss, as does the wind in sites where containers are exposed to every passing breeze. All this adds up to the need for regular watering, maybe as often as twice a day. However, if this is likely to be too onerous, there are plenty of solutions which include buying or making self-watering containers or installing an irrigation system (see pages 42-44).

Wind. Funnelling around buildings and whipping around corners, wind can batter fruit and foliage, break young growth, and blow away pollinating insects. Be sure to get familiar with your site, making the most of sheltered spots. Put up windbreaks if necessary, or avoid growing very soft-leaved plants that are easily damaged.

Ready-made products

Exciting developments in living walls worldwide have worked their way down to domestic level, so there are now many ready-made options for installing growing systems to clothe walls in part or full: handsome enough to grace town houses and apartments. Most of these 'living wall units' are best suited to the outdoors, though some models are designed as clean, self-contained units that enable plants to be grown indoors. New designs are popping up on a regular basis, so it's always worth looking out for the latest developments – though watch out for cheaper copies made from flimsier materials. The old adage of you get what you pay for tends to hold true, whatever you're buying.

Described here are various designs of ready-made unit that are suitable and straightforward for the individual to buy and install. There are companies that specialise in large-scale living wall installations up to

Matchmaking for success

While some plants are sunbathers that adore a hot site, others shrivel under a merciless blast of rays. Always make sure you match the right plant to the right place. For example, salad plants, most of which have lush leaves, prefer a part-shaded spot, whereas the majority of fruiting vegetables, fruit and herbs really thrive in the sun. Strawberries are a good example.

several storeys high, of the type now appearing in cities around the world, but these are certainly not for the DIY individual.

These growing systems are varied, but broadly speaking each design comes in small modules or units that can be put together and built up to create larger areas of planted wall. The slenderest designs comprise planting trays or modules that are attached to walls on metal frames or fixed on to battens, such as the VertiGarden. More substantial units comprise frameworks similar in structure to bookcases, but with v-shaped troughs or planting pockets, such as the Easiwall, which, again, is fitted to a wall using battens. Some designs walk a middle path between this style of living wall and a more traditional planter. An example is the Woolly Pocket, a felt-like material made into a series of hanging, modular planting pockets.

Buyer's checklist

- Does the supporting framework suit your site? Check whether your wall or fence is sufficiently sound and sturdy if you plan to fix units directly on to it. If in doubt, choose a design that is partly or fully floor-standing.
- Is the unit supplied complete with all necessary fixings? It's infuriating to get planters, compost and plants all ready and then find you haven't got any screws! You're likely to need a drill too.
- Does the unit incorporate a watering system, or is one offered as an optional extra? Adding your own irrigation system may add a substantial cost.
- What is it made of? Many units are made from recycled material such as PET plastic, which is more environmentally friendly.
- Is there a guarantee, and for how long?
- Is there enough rooting area for the food plants you want to grow? Some units are made of small modules that can only accommodate a limited range of plants.

Types of ready-made 'living wall units'

The examples given by name in this section are the main ones available in the UK at the moment – a more limited range than is available for familiar and long-established containers such as hanging baskets, window boxes and self-watering containers. Elsewhere, particularly in the USA, there is more choice. But the situation is changing all the time as businesses become aware of the huge potential of vertical growing, so keep an eye on gardening magazines and garden shows for the very latest developments.

Modular fabric planters

These can be found in a range of materials, designs and prices, so it's well worth weighing up the differences before you buy. They generally have eyelets in the top corners or at intervals along the top, which you simply hang on to large hooks or nails. The cheapest products are made from lightweight woven fabric which, it goes without saying, is not likely to be very durable. Should you want a planter that only lasts for one growing season, there is a biodegradable type that can be added to the compost bin at the end of the year, plants and all. Some fabric models are 'non-drip' and hence are suitable for indoors as well as outside. Check whether the eyelets are reinforced and also whether the higher planting pockets allow for effective 'filtering down' of water into the lower ones. Another example, the Verti-Plant, is pictured on page 2.

As well as material quality and durability, look at the pocket size and spacing: if the material is not attractive and the aim is to cover the

Wall units with tiered pockets, such as these 'Woolly Pockets', look attractive and usually offer a reasonable amount of rooting space.

panel as quickly as possible, larger pockets with closer spacing will give better results.

Modular panels: with planting pockets

Tiered panels made of rigid plastic are fixed to a wall or fence using wood or steel battens. Planting pockets protrude out from the panel and hence have two advantages over the flat modular panels (see overleaf): it is easy to replant while the panels are *in situ* and plants have a larger rooting area.

Individual panels are approximately 60cm (2') high and wide, and a number of them can be fixed adjacent to each other to create a seamless 'living wall'. Black is the most common colour, but white and terracotta are also available. Irrigation, which is generally optional, can be installed out of sight within the system. The 'Minigarden' design also includes base trays to catch the surplus water, so this design can be used indoors or out.

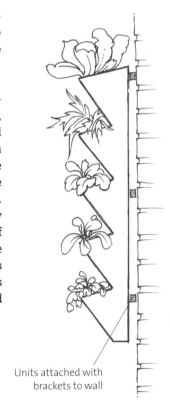

Units attached with brackets to wall

Modular panels: flat

Shallow modular panels made of rigid plastic can be used as single units or linked together to make large displays of any size. Each panel is approximately 60cm (2') high. Models such as the VertiGarden (pictured on page 49) comprise an outer metal frame, growing tray and lid plus a mesh top, and incorporate internal irrigation lines that are supplied from a separate tank sitting on top or from an additional irrigation system. The growing tray fits into the metal frame, which is fixed to the wall or other vertical surface.

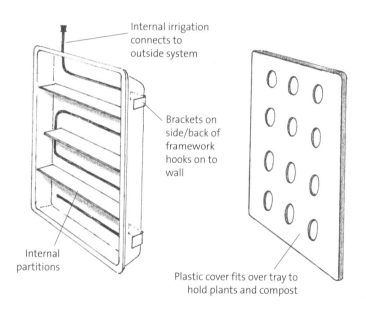

Internal irrigation connects to outside system

Brackets on side/back of framework hooks on to wall

Internal partitions

Plastic cover fits over tray to hold plants and compost

Stacking planters

As an alternative to fixing units to a vertical surface, choose containers that can be stacked so, although attached to a vertical support for stability, the lower ones can take at least some proportion of the weight, rather than the building, wall or fence. For a long, trough shape, the Modu-wall (pictured on page 63) is a sturdy design made of thick, rigid plastic. Inside the unit a thick layer of foam holds a reserve of water for plants to use. The slenderest type of planter is the Polanter, a cylindrical design made of rigid plastic, in a range of colours, with planting holes and incorporating a porous hose for watering. The rooting area is sufficient for growing salads, herbs, strawberries or small trailing tomatoes. Several planters can be placed on top of each other to form a tall cylinder. This design is not self-supporting and does need fixing to a vertical surface.

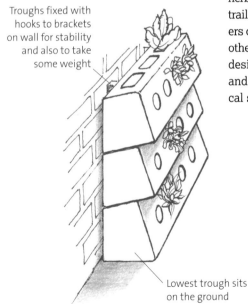

Troughs fixed with hooks to brackets on wall for stability and also to take some weight

Lowest trough sits on the ground

Troughs on a framework

The maximum area for rooting and growing is offered by the type of system that comprises troughs held on a vertical framework. The troughs may be either fixed or removable. This design is sometimes described as a 'vertical allotment', one example being the Easiwall, which comes in two sizes: the smaller unit is made up of five troughs, the larger one has an additional four plus horizontal trellis on top to support short climbing plants. Integral irrigation/self-watering troughs are optional.

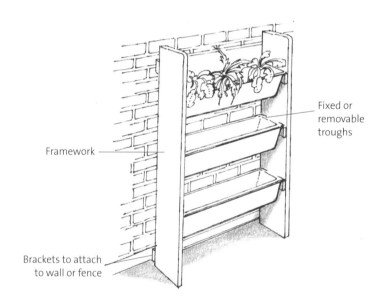

Fixed or removable troughs

Framework

Brackets to attach to wall or fence

This stackable model is the Modu-wall. The bottom unit can be placed on the ground and take the weight of the upper ones, or the units can be attached solely to the vertical surface.

How to plant ready-made 'living wall units'

The planting method varies according to whether the unit is 'flat' – with the soil and plants effectively at a right angle to the ground – or whether the plants are in pockets or troughs with the soil surface horizontal. Do read the instructions first (not as daft as it may sound – surveys show that many of us ignore the paperwork in our rush to get on with the job!) and be sure to thoroughly check any internal irrigation pipes. In addition to making sure that connections are secure and pipes sound, I like to run water through the system *before* filling it with compost and plants – potentially saving heaps of hassle in the unlikely event of there being a problem.

The truly vertical type of design, such as the VertiGarden, which is flat-fronted and so the plants are growing perpendicular to the ground, will need to be planted up while horizontal, i.e. before it is hung on the wall. It may give the choice of planting with young, plug plants or using larger plants in 9cm (3½") pots. If plug plants or indeed seedlings are used for planting up, the trays really should be kept horizontal for several weeks until growth is established, which will obviously leave gaps on your wall as well as requiring space for the units to be grown horizontally for that time. But if using larger well-established pot-grown plants, the modules can be hung up straight away, as the larger root ball of the plant stops soil washing out from the holes in the cover.

The majority of designs are of the pocket or trough type and can be planted up once the unit is *in situ* – best if the material is a flexible woven or fabric type. If it comprises troughs or containers hung on a rigid framework, the frame should be fixed in place first. Then the containers can be planted up and then lifted into place, or planted up once in position.

To plant up the flexible pocket type, hang up the container first and put a little compost in the base of the pockets to fill around a quarter to a third full, depending on the size of the root ball. Place the plants in the pocket so that the tops of the root balls are around a couple of centimetres below the rim. Carefully fill around the roots with more compost – a small scoop or a home-made one fashioned from a cut-down plastic bottle is useful for filling without making too much mess – and firm gently with your fingers, but take care not to press down hard on the compost as this squeezes out air spaces that are vital for healthy growth. The final compost level should be the same as the top of the root ball – creating a gap between soil and container rim allows for easy watering, as water can gather and then soak down, rather than running over the rim of the container and making a mess by washing out compost into the bargain.

Best plants for shallow containers

Modular living wall units and other containers that have a shallow rooting area (up to 15cm/6" wide and deep) must be partnered with crops that thrive in these growing conditions. The majority of these are salads, and many of the varieties below are 'cut and come again' crops, which means harvesting a few leaves at a time rather than taking whole plants in one fell swoop. This has a double benefit: plants remain small and hence more tolerant of shallow soil, while you have something attractive to look at for a long time, which is an important consideration for containers in high-profile sites.

- Cress: not just that old favourite, curled cress, but also Greek cress (spicier) and land cress.
- Lettuce: loose-leaf varieties and lamb's lettuce (also known as corn salad).
- Mixed salad leaves: available in many variety blends to suit all tastes.
- Mizuna: an oriental leafy vegetable sometimes included in salad leaf mixes.
- Pak choi: grow either as 'baby leaves' or as larger plants. For the latter, choose compact varieties such as 'Canton Dwarf'.
- Radicchio and leaf chicory (to pick young as salad leaves).
- Rocket: salad or cultivated varieties of rocket are better than wild rocket in small containers.
- Watercress: thrives so long as soil does not dry out.
- As well as leafy crops consider round-rooted carrots, beet to harvest as 'baby beet' and round-rooted radishes.
- Edible flowers look great and taste good too. Those that tolerate shallow soil include pot marigold, nasturtium and viola.
- Compact-growing herbs include basil, chives, golden marjoram, golden lemon balm, parsley and thyme.

Traditional containers

Simple containers in their many and varied forms have a huge amount to offer the small-space verti-gardener. Window boxes, hanging baskets and variations on these such as mangers and half-baskets (literally half a hanging basket that sits flat against its support) are all useful, traditional and reasonably priced ways of growing plants on vertical surfaces. Even lower in cost are hanging growing bags, sold under a variety of names such as flower bags, pouches or swags. All these different containers can, with a little thought and ingenuity, be positioned and planted to give a steady supply of produce, conveniently ready to hand right near the door.

With an ever-increasing selection to choose from, the two questions to ask yourself to start with are: (a) how much do I want to spend and (b) how smart does it need to look? In a prime spot – say, next to the front door, or in a balcony or courtyard that is your only outdoor space – you may feel that it's worth spending a bit more, either in terms of time, effort and creativity, or in cash, so your outside space looks smart for all or much of the year. Quirky and fun recycled containers (see page 74) can make a great display too: bear in mind that even those which are less than handsome can be edged with trailing plants that will soon cascade down and hide the humble origins of their home.

Hanging baskets

Easily suspended from brackets, hooks or railings, hanging baskets can grow a surprisingly substantial harvest. There is a range of basket designs: some are designed to be ornamental, some more functional, the cheapest of which is the traditional open-mesh type. While this offers most potential for ornament, as the sides and base can be planted as well as the top to truly maximise growing space, the downsides are

Best plants for hanging baskets

Baskets do come in a variety of sizes, but in most cases you'll have a greater depth and area of soil to play with than shallower containers such as ready-made living wall units (although all the plants mentioned in the box on page 65 can be grown in hanging baskets too). There are many potential plant combinations – a lettuce medley using different types of loose-leaf or cut-and-come-again varieties; or a herb

Trailing tomatoes make fabulous hanging-basket plants. This variety is 'Tumbling Tom Red'.

collection of kitchen favourites such as chives and parsley with trailing golden marjoram and thymes around the sides. But if you're new to gardening or just prefer the simple life, the easiest way to create an edible basket is to fill it with just one type of plant from the list below – these are bushy yet trailing to at least some degree, so they 'fill' the basket in a pleasing way. These suggested quantities are for a medium-sized (35cm/14") diameter basket.

- Trailing tomatoes: three plants per basket.
- Strawberries: six plants.
- Chilli and sweet peppers: three plants.
- Bushy and compact-growing courgettes: only one of these vigorous plants.
- Bush nasturtiums: six plants.

a high level of water loss and also the need for lining (preferably not with sphagnum moss, which is harvested from fast-dwindling bogs, but with a recycled alternative such as coir or a wool-based liner). Solid-based hanging baskets may not have the same amount of planting space but are much easier to maintain as they retain more moisture. Self-watering designs (see pages 44 and 74) incorporate a water reservoir and hence are even better from this point of view.

Window boxes

Window boxes have an ultra-traditional and perhaps slightly dull image, but these old favourites have a huge amount to offer the gardener. Apartment-dwellers, in particular, take note – one great advantage of window boxes that is worth considering is that you can maintain and harvest produce from indoors as well as out, making the most of spots that can't be accessed from the ground. They are perfect for herbs, edible flowers, salad leaves and mini-greens when you just want to grab a few leaves to flavour or garnish a dish.

Another key consideration with window boxes is that they can be cheap! Older-style plastic troughs can often be picked up for a song from jumble or car boot sales, while I've had some great ones for nothing via the web-based organisation Freecycle (www.freecycle.org), which is dedicated to keeping reusable stuff out of landfill sites. Or if you're handy with a saw, hammer and nails, it's quite straightforward to make your own (see opposite). Of course there are plenty of ready-made designs available, including self-watering models that incorporate a water reservoir and hence offer the opportunity to significantly cut down on maintenance.

The long, narrow troughs typically sold for windows can be fitted on to vertical surfaces in all kinds of ways. Of course if you have wide, deep sills, just sit a trough there and plant up a display that looks good from both indoors and out. If your windows are sill-less, simply screw sturdy L-shaped brackets just beneath the window on which to sit a box. Consider the second option if the first one means you can't open your windows: more than a bit of a drawback, to say the least. Develop the bracket idea, though, and the possibilities unfold. Why not a rank of troughs on brackets, marching up a wall, secured to a stout trellis panel, or up a fence, or suspended from railings? Indeed, if you have a balcony or railings, there are now window boxes designed with a recess running underneath along the box, so it can sit securely on top with the railing in the recess.

A canny way to keep your boxes looking good for all or much of the time – and to grow even more crops – is to buy an inner box liner (or make your own from strong geotextile membrane, sold as ground cover or weed-control fabric). Yet another option is to buy cheap plastic troughs to sit inside smart ones. The liner can be planted up with young plants or seeds and grown on in an out-of-the-way corner, ready to be dropped into the main window box as soon as the previous occupants have finished cropping.

Make your own window box

Old planks can be turned into handsome plant boxes with a little DIY skill and an attractive coloured wood stain – one that is non-toxic to plants, obviously. The great advantage of building your own box is that the design can be made to exactly fit your site; if size isn't important, go for a minimum length of 60cm (2') and a height/depth of 25cm (10"). Drill several 2cm (¾") drainage holes in the base so water can drain freely. Fix together using galvanised nails (these won't rust) and paint the box both inside and out using a suitable stain or preservative.

Safety first

Security and stability must be an absolute priority for window boxes above ground-floor level. Even if your sills are wide and the box appears to be sitting comfortably, ensure boxes are firmly fixed by hammering a couple of vine eyes (stainless steel fixings sold for securing climbers to walls) to the inner corners of the sill. Before planting up the box, at each end pass a length of wire through the inside and out via the drainage holes and then thread through the vine eyes when the trough is put in place. If your windowsill has a pronounced slope, slot wedges under the front edge of the box for stability.

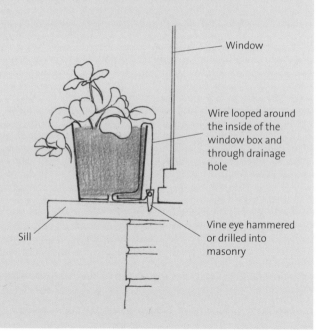

Window

Wire looped around the inside of the window box and through drainage hole

Vine eye hammered or drilled into masonry

Sill

Best-looking herbs for containers

Herbs are immensely versatile and often compact-growing plants that have the potential to grow almost anywhere – ideal, of course, for small containers such as window boxes, hanging baskets and living wall units, as well as larger containers. Because herbs often occupy a high-profile spot – such as outside the kitchen window, handy to harvest – it's good to choose varieties that look great for much if not all of the year. The following herbs head up the league of good-lookers:

- Basil with purple or frilled leaves (frost tender so summer only)
- Curly-leaved parsley
- Chives and garlic chives
- Golden and purple sage
- Golden marjoram
- Golden lemon balm
- Mints with variegated leaves such as apple mint (grow mint in a sunken, bottomless pot or it will take over the whole container)
- Thymes with gold or variegated leaves
- Trailing rosemary

Window-box herbs are the ultimate in convenience gardening.

Hanging growing 'bags'

Mention 'growing bag' or 'growbag' and most people think of the type placed on the ground, usually home to tomatoes or cucumbers. While these are good for climbing plants (see below), there are growing bags designed to hang from on high. These tough plastic or woven polypropylene bags, sold under various names such as Flower Pouch or Flower Tower, are a useful and inexpensive way to hang up plants in awkward spots, because they can be simply tied on using wire or placed on a hook. One drawback is that effective and thorough watering can be hard to achieve when there is only a small surface area of compost in relation to the container depth, as the water can easily run off rather than penetrate deep down. Avoid the problem in the first place by inserting a piece of soaker hose or perforated tube prior to planting, which will channel the water down into the lower part of the container. Some designs are supplied with this sort of watering device.

Hanging bags and flower pouches are ideal for awkward spots such as drainpipes. This one gave a good harvest of mizuna for several months.

Hanging plant bags are designed to be planted up with seedlings or little plug plants, because to plant larger pot-grown ones would mean cutting a hole so big it would destabilise the container. A common mistake is to plant and hang up bags immediately, resulting in something akin to an internal landslip where the plants and compost shift just a bit in response to gravity. Though not enough to stop the plants from growing, it's usually sufficient to expose the fabric of the container in places so it looks unattractive. To grow great-looking hanging bags, plan to sow or plant under cover where the container can be left lying down for several weeks so the root systems become well established. Only then should you hang it up, and gravity will soon do its bit to get plant growth draping elegantly down.

Best plants for hanging bags

The rooting space within a hanging growing bag is very limited and will quickly become congested with roots, but even in this challenging environment there is still a fair choice of plants that can be grown. Here are just a few ideas:

- Herbal tea 'bag': chamomile growing through the sides, Moroccan mint bushing out the top. Or peppermint planted through the sides with lemon balm on the top.
- Salad bag: any of the many blends of mixed salad leaves, plus a few violas to give colour both when growing and so the blooms can be picked to decorate a salad bowl.
- Colourful nasturtiums: bring a bolt of brilliant colour to a sunny spot with this easy and multipurpose annual. Both the leaves and flowers can be added to salads, while seeds can be pickled and used like capers.
- Minty breath: common mint is renowned for its thuggish growing tendencies, so keeping it in isolation is the perfect solution.
- Succulent strawberries: grow a perpetual-fruiting type such as 'Mara des Bois', which will give you a few delectable fruits to pick little and often over a long period.

'Self-watering' containers

Several types of container including hanging baskets, troughs and pots include models that are 'self-watering', which in this case means a built-in water reservoir in the base from which the plants draw up water as required (as illustrated on page 44). This design incorporates a divider that ensures that the soil and roots are separated from the water yet are still in constant contact, preventing waterlogging while still ensuring a good supply of essential oxygen to the roots.

A well-designed self-watering container has an easily accessible fill point and must have an overflow facility to avoid water building up during periods of high rainfall. This type is especially good for plants that need a steady supply of moisture to produce a good crop, such as tomatoes which suffer from various conditions such as fruit split and blossom end rot if water supply is erratic. Self-watering containers are said to produce higher yields because as the plants lose water from their leaves and draw it up via their roots – a process known as transpiration – so there is always a supply available (as long as you remember to top up the reservoir, that is!). One important point to remember is that when this type of container is first planted, the root system has yet to establish to the point where the plant can draw up water. You will need to water from the top for at least several weeks.

For instructions on to make your own self-watering plastic bottle container, see page 78.

Making your own containers

When a plethora of recycled garden features have become a firmly established part of the prestigious Chelsea Flower Show, eco-friendly gardens have definitely made it into the realm of fashion. Giving throw-away items a new life in your garden does a real 'double whammy' good turn for both the environment and your pocket. Rubbish takes on a whole new perspective when viewed as prospective plant containers: after all, anything that holds compost and can have holes made in it for drainage is fair game for planting up in my book. My long-suffering family is almost (though not quite) inured to the embarrassment of trudging back from the beach laden with washed-up fish boxes (ideal as they have stout handles for hanging up) and anything else plant-able, but just keep a weather eye around your locality. Car boot or jumble sales, even skips (though ask the owner before rummaging) are likely to turn up suitable 'hangables' while Freecycle often comes up trumps with rich pickings. Here are just a few ideas; let your imagina-tion run and you're bound to come up with more.

- Bird cages: smaller ones are designed to hang up but remember that the weight of compost, plants and water is far heavier than a budgie or parrot. Add a stout metal hook, such as the type used for hanging up kitchen utensils. Note that any wire or mesh cages, plus other items detailed below, will need some sort of liner to retain compost. This can be done in the same way as lining a hanging basket (see page 66).
- Pet cages made out of wire such as rat or hamster cages. Being larger and therefore heavier means they may need stronger support such as brackets below, instead of (or as well as) a hook for hanging up.
- Vegetable racks. Wall-mounted types consisting of several plastic or mesh trays make superb plant containers. The plastic type that just has a few holes in the base of each tray won't need a full lining; just place a kitchen cloth in the bottom of each tray before planting to prevent watery compost seeping out the bottom.
- Garden incinerators made of mesh. Most are tall and fairly narrow – ideal for potatoes or deep-rooted plants such as runner beans,

courgettes or carrots. The larger size makes this type of container impractical to hang up, but ideal for standing at the base of a wall. Consider stacking two or even three on top of each other, if this can be done securely – by running a couple of long steel rods inside the stack, for example.

- Catering-sized food cans (from school canteens or similar). These look gorgeous when painted and offer the opportunity to be creative with different designs and colours too. To hang up, punch a hole near the rim using a hammer and large nail (put a block of wood inside the tin first so it doesn't bend out of shape) and slip in a loop of strong wire that can be easily slipped on to a hook or nail on the wall or fence.

- Hanging shoe storers, wardrobe organisers or bedside storage caddies. These are great ready-made 'growing bags' if made of a sufficiently strong material: fabric is excellent, but avoid light-weight polythene ones that won't take much weight or will degrade quickly when exposed to sunlight. Dye light-coloured ones a darker colour, as pale fabric quickly discolours and looks horrid when planted up. Hang on nails or strong hooks.

- Stout shopping bags, either canvas, jute or fabric. These too can be made into ready-made growing bags: the same points apply as above. However, because they have greater capacity while also needing to be filled almost up to the top, mitigate the weight by half-filling with chunks of polystyrene before adding compost.

Fish boxes rescued from the beach are great for growing many kinds of fruit and veg.

DIY self-watering plastic bottle containers

Plastic bottles are a waste nightmare but a gardener's dream. Large clear plastic bottles have loads of uses, but this one – as mini-containers with their own water reservoirs – is my favourite by far, particularly as it tackles the problem of plants that dry out fast in small containers. See overleaf for step-by-step instructions. While I can't claim the bottle planter as my original idea, the 'living wall' design using trellis, pictured here, is all mine. Making plastic bottle containers is a great project for children of any age too, so long as adults do the hot and sharp bits. Depending on weather and site conditions, plants are likely to need watering only once a week or so. Do check from time to time, though, to make sure the 'wick' is touching the water or plants will dry out very quickly.

You will need:
- Bottles, minimum 2-litre (3½-pint) size, rinsed out and with screw tops and labels removed.
- Capillary matting (available off the roll from garden centres and DIY stores). Failing that, a bit of woollen fabric will do.
- String.
- Sharp scissors.
- Soldering iron (preferably) or skewer/screwdriver for making holes.

Create a living wall of bottle planters using two pieces of trellis, one slightly higher than the other.

How to make a self-watering plastic bottle container

1. Cut the bottle in half. (If you're using ordinary scissors, pinch the bottle in order to cut easily.)
2. Cut a small square of capillary matting and tie it securely over the mouth.
3. Heat the soldering iron or skewer and use it to make around half a dozen holes for drainage, close to the neck of the bottle.
4. Invert the top part to fit snugly inside the lower half. Your bottle is now ready for planting.

The recycler's checklist

To successfully adapt 'pre-loved' items into plant containers, run through these guidelines first:

- Is it strong enough? Even lightweight potting compost can be heavy when wet, and you need to add on the weight of mature plants. If the hanging loop looks a bit flimsy, fix on or sew a stronger one. Alternatively, substitute with metal kitchen utensil hooks – a great way to hang up all kinds of containers.

- Can the water drain out, or can drainage holes be made? Water must be able to drain or the roots will stagnate and die, so be sure you can make holes that won't compromise the container's strength.

- How thick is it, does it need extra insulation? Adding an insulating layer inside is often necessary with thin-walled items. Watch out for metal in particular – it makes plant roots over-hot in summer and cold in winter. Insulate the sides (but not the base) with bubble wrap, cardboard or thick wedges of newspaper.

- Does it need lining to hold compost in? For mesh and open-weave containers, use a hanging basket lining material to retain compost.

- How long will it last? Materials such as fabric or polythene are likely to degrade fairly fast and may only last for one growing season.

Climbing plants

A traditional, straightforward and great-looking way to make the most of any vertical surface is by planting tall-growing, trainable or climbing plants at the base, to be tied on to a support of some kind so they tightly clothe as much of the area as possible. Of course the growing is easiest where plants can go in border soil, but lack of ground need not be a bar as plants can be grown in containers of many types.

All climbing vegetables and fruit benefit from pots at least 30cm (1') high, because most form deep root systems. Long-lived plants such as vines, berry and tree fruit need larger containers, up to a half-barrel size if you can. If weight isn't an issue, always use soil-based (John Innes type) potting compost because these long-lived plants are likely to occupy their container for years and need substantial top quality compost in order to perform well. Make sure the container can withstand winter frosts if housing a permanent plant.

How plants climb

In order to decide which support or framework to provide, it's immensely useful to distinguish between the ways that plants climb. Indeed, many so-called 'climbers' do not 'climb' at all but are simply tall and lanky growers in need of support, or are amenable enough to being pulled about to adapt to a space-saving lifestyle, flat against a framework. I strongly recommend putting up any supports before planting – putting them up later can be a lot of hassle and cause damage.

True climbers either wind their stems around something in order to grow upwards, or scramble up 'hand over hand' by means of tendrils or winding leaf stems. For example, beans fall into the first category, pumpkins and peas the latter. Hence, 'winders' such as beans do best on poles or a fan-trained arrangement, whereas tendril climbers prefer trellis (so long as the wood is sufficiently thin for the tendrils to wind around – which varies according to the plant) or some form of diamond or square mesh. 'Leaners', for want of a better term, that need tying to or training up a support, include tomatoes, cucumbers, currant and berry fruits, grapes, kiwi-fruit and trained fruit trees.

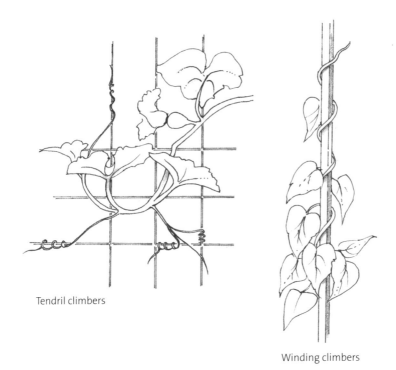

Tendril climbers

Winding climbers

Combination growing

It's easy to fall into the trap of thinking we have to grow one way or the other, either by having climbing or trainable plants on a vertical surface, or by covering the area with containers, be they living wall units or a more traditional type. To get the very most from a wall or fence, though, a combination of both methods is likely to be most productive. Containers mounted on walls and fences can be fixed either high or low, depending on the growth habit of the climbing plant and where the training system is fixed. Many climbing and wall plants tend to have 'bare ankles' with stems that have little or no growth on the lower part, which leaves space near the base. Another option is to create the supporting frameworks with spaces in between for containers such as wall baskets, troughs or living wall units.

Best climbing fruit

Even the smallest space can grow a whole host of delectable, succulent, vitamin-packed fresh fruit, because the vast majority of varieties can be adapted to vertical growing in different ways. Sun for at least half the day is essential to achieve a reasonable crop.

- 'Flexible' berry fruits such as blackberries, loganberries or tayberries can be trained and tied on to any framework such as wires or trellis. Thornless varieties are preferable, for obvious reasons.
- Raspberries form tall canes that can be tied to any vertical frame.
- Marvellously vigorous climbers such as grape vines and kiwi fruit happily spread over a wide wall or fence – they will be equally happy to go up and over a pergola, arch or arbour.
- Blackcurrants, redcurrants and whitecurrants can be grown as cordons with straight, single or double stems.
- Tree fruits can be bought pre-trained to different shapes: as single-stemmed cordons to plant at 45-degree angles; as fans; or as espalier (tiered) shapes.
- There's even a 'climbing' strawberry that can be trained up a support – a variety called 'Mount Everest'.

Check the small print when buying fruit, as some types need to be pollinated by another of the same type in order to produce a crop. If you're limited to only one plant, make sure you choose a variety that is self-fertile.

Best climbing veg

- Beans may be frost tender, but that's usually the only tricky thing about them. Otherwise these twining climbers are easy to grow and produce masses of pods for months. Runner and climbing French beans have attractive flowers: especially pretty are the red-and-white 'Painted Lady' and cream-and-white 'White Emergo'. Some French beans have colourful pods, for example the yellow 'Corona d'Oro' and purple 'Violet Podded Stringless'. There's also the pretty and unusual hyacinth bean (also known as dolichos or lablab bean).

Many vegetables, such as the mangetout pea 'Shiraz', look as good as they taste.

- Peas are easy to grow, reaching out their tendrils to rapidly scramble up trellis or mesh. Mangetout are more attractive than traditional types, especially varieties such as 'Shiraz'. Peas tolerate cold more than beans so can be sown outside from mid-spring.

- Cucurbits – pumpkins, marrows and squashes – form a large and diverse group of varieties with wonderfully colourful and decorative fruit. Vigour varies enormously, so check that your chosen variety fits your space. As the fruit swells, you may need to support the larger ones: I make 'hammocks' out of old tights or fishing net.

- Tall varieties of tomatoes and cucumbers need to be supported on stakes, trellis, wires or anything similar.

Supporting your climbing plants

Climbing and wall-trained plants usually need sturdy supports in order to sustain the weight of mature plants – which hopefully will be loaded with a good crop too. Flimsy trellis or bamboo canes are rarely strong enough.

When climbers and trained plants are to be grown on existing walls and fences, the easiest and most economical support is made using stout galvanised wires, run through vine eyes (metal screws with a loop through which to run the wire). The hammer-in type is easier to

Large, deep containers such as this recycled zinc tub are ideal for deep-rooted vegetables: in this case runner beans and golden courgette.

install than screw-in ones, which need drilling and possibly the addition of wall plugs. Depending on the growth habit of your chosen climbers, the wires need to be either placed in a fan shape or spaced horizontally 23-30cm (9-12") apart. This framework should last for years and provide an unobtrusive means of support.

Trellis is excellent as a free-standing screen, on a boundary or within a garden, and can look very decorative. Styles vary from simple and less costly squared trellis to diamonds or squares with wide battens: generally the more wood in the design, the higher the cost. A wide choice of coloured wood stains can be used to turn trellis into decorative garden features. Do bear in mind that it will need treating every 2-3 years to keep it in good condition. Should you use trellis fixed directly to a wall or fence, place 2.5-5cm (1-2") wooden battens between the two, which gives stems sufficient room to twine around them.

When it comes to those plants that lean, such as tomatoes, any sturdy post, trellis, even rope will do the job of support. To avoid growth slipping down its support, I adapt whatever I'm using to suit: by hammering in a few large nails to a post, for example, or tying loops at 15cm (6") intervals along a rope.

Free-standing obelisks, wigwams and other features can also be used to support climbers, either when growing in containers or against walls and fences. There's plenty of opportunity here to make your own – here are just some of my favourite ideas:

- Willow and hazel wigwam. Make your own from growth harvested (or bought) when dormant. Select straight, sturdy hazel branches to the desired height (including the length to be inserted into the container) and place in the soil. This is easiest to do when the container is full of soil/compost, but before planting. Use young, pliable willow stems to weave two or three horizontal bands around the uprights. Both willow and hazel are easy to grow: if you have space, grow one of each and 'coppice' annually or every second year by cutting all growth back almost to ground level.

- A single stout post made of timber at least 7.5cm (3") square. Hammer in a dozen or so 10-15cm (4-6") long nails and make a 'spider's web' of twine or string, or surround with netting, for plants to climb up.

- A 'maypole' design using a post or stake as a centrepiece, with half a dozen stout wires, string or slender ropes leading down to the ground and pegged into the soil. I like to secure the ends to an old bicycle wheel trim, if the container is large enough.

A willow and hazel wigwam.

- Bamboo canes. Simple, quick and easy. Insert the ends to a depth of at least 15-23cm (6-9") and tie together at the top.

CHAPTER 3

Green roofs

A green or 'living' roof has huge potential to transform a building into a feature that is both attractive and productive. In towns and cities, access to a roof and the ability to grow plants in any way possible is an incredible opportunity to create your own living haven: to harvest fresh produce when surrounded by concrete and tarmac. Recent developments in waterproofing membranes and lightweight growing medium have made it

possible to create green roofs on any scale, from huge projects such as Eagle Street Rooftop Farm in New York to small growing areas on individual roofs and balconies. While roof gardening is costly and harder compared to growing plants in the ground, it is immensely worthwhile where this is the only opportunity to garden and have at least a taste of fresh home-grown produce.

What's in a name?

It is useful to define commonly used terms for growing plants on roofs, in particular to clearly differentiate between a 'green roof' and a 'roof garden'.

A **green (or living) roof** is used to describe any roof site, be it flat or pitched (sloping), that has a layer of soil or other growing medium added in order for plants to grow and thrive. On a green roof, most or all of the area is covered with soil and vegetation, usually to a relatively shallow depth due to the substantial accumulated weight of the growing medium plus plants and water. The terms *living roof* or *eco-roof* tend to be used when the main aim of the site is that of habitat creation, enticing wildlife and boosting biodiversity. A green roof can be of any size: from a garage, shed, carport, bicycle shelter (or even a bird table) to whole roofs that cover all or part of a home.

A **roof garden** is where plants are grown in raised beds or containers and is often used to describe a space that could be large and includes paths, seating, decking and even lawns, while at the other end of the scale it can be as small as a balcony. For more on roof gardens see Chapter 4.

'Roof gardens' can come in all shapes and sizes. Here a household storage box has been adapted, with minimal drainage holes, to grow a good crop of watercress.

Get good advice

A green or living roof looks spectacular on a large scale but also works very well in many smaller-scale situations too: where homeowners are stuck with utilitarian garden buildings such as sheds, garages and carports, changing the covering to a growing one can transform the entire outside area. If the situation is such that apartments or reverse-level accommodation directly overlook the roof, the results can be truly stunning. However, practical considerations such as waterproofing and weight loading must be absolutely paramount in order to ensure the security and long-term health of the building. If you are contemplating a larger project, whether you're looking at a green roof for a new building or retrofitting on to an existing one, using a specialist green roof contractor is very strongly recommended. The contractor will ensure the building can take the load, satisfy the building regulations and usually provide a long-term warranty so long as the installation conditions have been met.

Now green roofs are 'fashionable', no doubt there will be businesses jumping on the bandwagon and so it will really pay to do some sound research. Find a company with experience, which specialises in green roofs, ideally one which also has past examples of work to inspect and references to supply. In 2011, the Green Roof Organisation produced the first Green Roof Code for the UK, intended as a code of best practice relating to green roof design, specification, installation and maintenance (see www.greenroofcode.co.uk).

Good reasons to have a green roof

Green or living roofs deliver a whole range of benefits, both on a directly personal level and to the wider environment. Although some of the points on this list – such as boosting biodiversity, carbon sequestration and flood reduction – may seem ambitiously grand, never overlook the accretion of marginal gains. While one green roof may not make a difference, twenty, a hundred, or a thousand or more green roofs will start to make an appreciable contribution. One of my favourite quotes, attributed to several famous people including the Dalai Lama and Anita Roddick, is "If you think you're too small to make a difference, you've never been in bed with a mosquito."! With so much gloom and doom in the news, doing anything positive to redress the balance gives a huge boost to the morale.

Food production

Of course this is top of the list, given the focus of this book. When the only way is up, rooftops have incredible potential to grow a wide range of edible crops. Truly inspirational examples are springing up worldwide, such as Eagle Street Rooftop Farm in New York and the roof garden on Budgens supermarket in Crouch End, London (pictured on page 13).

Insulation and cooling

Our weather has changed dramatically over the last decade in particular, with periods of heat, drought, rain and cold becoming more unpredictable and intense. Thick roofs can help mitigate these extremes and have potential for reducing power consumption for both heating and air conditioning. A green roof not only insulates the building beneath, but in summer the water evaporating from the plants and growing medium helps cool the air around it. The term 'urban heat island' is used to describe a phenomenon whereby cities and towns are several degrees warmer than the surrounding countryside, owing to vast expanses of hard surfaces, lack of vegetation and the large proportion of dark, heat-absorbing surfaces, including roofs. The adoption of green roofs on a large scale can thereby help cool the urban environment.

Lowering pollution levels

Hotter urban environments not only result in more air pollution as more energy is used for air conditioning, but the heat creates low-level ozone, which is dangerous to health: produced when pollutants combine in the presence of heat and sunlight. Absorbing water (see the following point) also reduces other forms of pollution: that caused by storm water run-off, which becomes contaminated with a wide range of pollutants such as agricultural chemicals, road salt, tyre residues and oil. High levels of storm water often cause sewerage systems to overflow too.

Reducing rainwater run-off

As the earth's atmosphere warms, the air becomes more humid and periods of rain are being seen to increase in both frequency and severity, resulting in a greater incidence of flooding. In towns and cities with ever-increasing proportions of non-porous surfaces, sustainable urban drainage systems (SUDS) are the subject of much discussion. The effects are already being felt by ordinary homeowners: in the UK, paving over urban front gardens with non-permeable material now requires planning permission. Transforming any hard-surfaced area into a growing site helps slow the run-off process: soil or green roof growing medium has sponge-like capabilities, soaking up much of the water that falls, with the greater proportion never making it to ground level. Rainwater can also be gathered and stored from any building, to use for watering plants during dry spells.

Protecting and extending the life of a roof

Exposed to the elements, roofs are subject to extremes: harsh winds, winter frost and summer heat, especially the damaging effects of ultra-violet (UV) rays in sunlight. Snuggled under the 'duvet' of a green roof, protected from human activity as well as the elements, roof life can be substantially prolonged. Based on studies of roofs in Germany, one of the first countries where green roofs were installed, it is emerging that roof life is doubling and even tripling. Researchers at Nottingham Trent University found that while a conventional roof experienced temperature fluctuations of 30°C (86°F), under a green roof this reduced to less than 13°C (55°F).

Creating wildlife habitats and boosting biodiversity

The benefit to food gardeners is that many crops are insect-pollinated, primarily by bees, so their presence helps ensure a good crop. Transforming any bare surface into a living one will carry big benefits for biodiversity. Soil teems with microorganisms, and creatures of all sizes are attracted to plants – some desirable, such as bees, moths and butter-flies; others, such as slugs and snails, are less desirable from a food gardener's point of view. However, bear in mind that even these 'undesir-ables' are useful in providing food for beneficial creatures such as birds that predate on garden pests and help the gardener to achieve a balance of nature without resorting to harmful chemicals.

Improved solar panel performance

Panel efficiency reduces once the temperature rises above 25°C (77°F). By minimising temperature fluctuation on the roof and creating a more equable microclimate, a green roof can boost performance.

Sound insulation

Little research has been done on this subject to date, but adding to the bulk of walls and roofs will certainly reduce sound transmission to some extent. In our increasingly overcrowded world, cutting down on noise pollution can help to reduce stress, which comes with a whole host of attendant issues.

Carbon sequestration

The process of photosynthesis, by which plants take up carbon dioxide and give out oxygen, helps to reduce the growing amount of carbon in the earth's atmosphere. It goes without saying that a small amount of green roof would have little effect, but the impact would be greater on a large scale as there would be a correspondingly higher level of sequestered carbon.

Good looks

It may be hard to quantify the benefits, but never underestimate the boost to morale of seeing islands of green in a sea of concrete.

Types of green roof

There are three main types of green roof, categorised according to depth of planting medium (this term is used rather than 'soil', which is usually far too heavy to put on a roof).

- Intensive. Most like a conventional roof garden, with deep beds that can grow a wide range of plants.
- Semi-intensive. A growing medium up to 15cm (6") deep gives reasonable potential to grow edible plants.
- Extensive. A thin layer of growing medium, which can be as little as 5cm (2"), supports a very limited range of drought-tolerant plants; by far the most commonly used are sedums: tough, fleshy-leaved succulents (though of course these are not edible).

'Mix and match' roofs

There is no need for a roof to fall into one exact category. Providing there is sufficient weight-bearing capacity, a roof can be a mixture of shallow growing medium with deeper areas of soil made by creating soil mounds. Another option is raised beds, troughs or other containers that could be incorporated to provide a greater soil depth.

Modular roofs

A modular green roof is yet another option and is a good DIY approach, allowing the creation of a roof that appears to be growing all over, yet which can be changed in part or which allows access to the roof beneath. Perhaps the best way to describe this is as 'Lego' gardening! Here the planting is done into wide, shallow trays – great if there is the possibility of scrounging unwanted trays from a baker or supermarket, for example. The trays are set out side by side, filled with growing medium and then the joins concealed – also using a thin layer of growing medium.

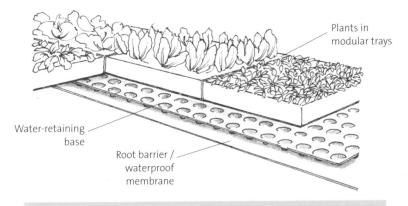

Plants in modular trays

Water-retaining base

Root barrier / waterproof membrane

A modular green roof, comprising separate trays, is easy to adapt or update.

Green roof construction practicalities

Although this is not intended as a detailed guide to green roofs, the following is an overview of the key points. See the Resources section for a couple of examples of books devoted to the subject.

Weight

This is without question the most important consideration with any green roof or roof garden. Never, ever underestimate the weight – not just of the growing medium and plants, but also when the roof is at saturation point with water: even the thinner type of green roof can weigh up to around 85kg per square metre (17lb per square foot), while a deeper roof of around 10cm (4") can be more than double that. If the roof will be used regularly by people, this needs to be taken into account too. A new-build structure is comparatively straightforward because it can be designed to suit, but retrofitting a green roof to an existing building must be done with care.

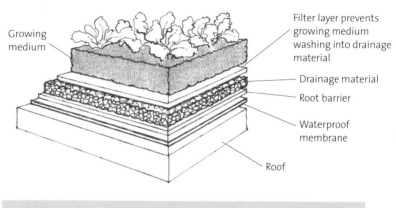

Growing medium

Filter layer prevents growing medium washing into drainage material

Drainage material

Root barrier

Waterproof membrane

Roof

Construction of a green roof.

Small-scale DIY projects, such as making a green roof on a garden shed or store, still need to be done with care. A building with timber walls is likely to need bracing, either internally from corner to corner, potentially with extra supporting beams over doors and windows too, or with bracing fitted to the outside. For more information on how to do this, I suggest referring to one of the books listed in the Resources section, such as *Small Green Roofs*.

Waterproofing layer

This is an immensely important part of a green roof which can only be touched on briefly here (see the Resources section for further sources of information). There are a number of choices of material for water-proofing a roof, principally a range of membranes and products applied in a liquid state. For small DIY projects, good-quality pond liner such as EPDM of a minimum thickness of 1.5mm can be used. Whatever material is used, it must be suitable for installation under a green roof.

Root barrier

This may not be necessary, as some waterproofing materials are inherently root-resistant. However, if not, it is important to install a geotextile root barrier fabric to prevent any possibility of roots piercing the waterproofing layer.

Drainage

A range of different materials can be used for a drainage layer, installed beneath the growing medium to prevent water building up on the roof. These include polystyrene, plastic, foam and crushed recycled waste such as brick or porcelain. There are also rigid plastic drainage bases that are 'honeycombed' with small depressions that provide a water reservoir that plants can draw on when necessary.

Filter layer

Depending on the other materials used, it may be advisable to add a layer of water-permeable fabric that prevents the growing medium washing down and clogging up the drainage layer. It is also important that there is no danger of the growing medium also seeping into gutters and blocking these, the downpipes or ground drains.

Growing medium

Instead of soil, which is generally too heavy to use on roofs and other weight-critical locations, use a growing medium that has been specifically made for a green roof so as to be lightweight yet with optimum levels of air, moisture retention, nutrient supply and drainage, and one that also has a structure that does not break down over time. Typical substrates are made of a mix of aggregates, such as crushed brick, and a relatively low percentage of organic matter – as little as 10 per cent for extensive roofs. Those containing a substantial proportion of recycled material should conform to British Standards ref. BAS PAS 100.

Green roof gardening practicalities

The key practical points of gardening off the ground are outlined in Chapter 1, but the most important one that certainly bears repeating is safety – the first and by far the most important aspect of gardening on a roof. It is vital that any raised area has a secure barrier all around; if children are to use the area at all, the barrier must be sufficiently high or un-climbable. Any access in the form of steps, staircases, ladders and so on must also be securely fixed with suitable handrails.

Once this essential is covered, the more pleasurable aspects of the actual gardening can be addressed. When choosing the types of tools to be used, and what they're made from, do consider the potential effects on the underlying roof structure and hence avoid anything that could pierce or damage it. Where larger hand tools are required, for example, opt for a spade rather than a sharp-tined, membrane-piercing fork and a plastic-tined rake over a metal one. On a smaller and similar scale, a trowel is preferable to a fork and a little swan-neck or 'onion' hoe gives more control than a long-handled type.

To minimise the work of carting things on to and off the roof, try to build in some storage for tools and equipment: a large plastic or wooden storage box is ideal. For the same reason, aim to recycle waste *in situ* too. Small amounts can be composted in a wormery, which turns waste into rich compost and also produces a liquid plant food. For slightly larger quantities of waste, my favoured option is a wormery/composter hybrid such as the 'Green Johanna'. Both of these are vermin-proof and can compost cooked food scraps along with garden waste.

As mentioned earlier, water is another key consideration as roofs are exposed to sun and wind and plants will dry out much faster than on the ground. Make sure that there is a good supply of water to hand, then be prepared either to water by hand on a regular basis or set up a watering system to do the job for you. If the latter, do remember to check it from time to time, though – systems are not infallible.

Growing plants on green roofs

Growing vegetables and other edibles directly on a green roof is still very much in its infancy. A roof can be a surprisingly harsh environment, exposed to the full force of wind, sun and rain, and hence drying out far faster than growing areas on the ground or in more sheltered spots. Without extra protection in the form of shading or screening to filter the wind and sun, many vegetable and fruit plants will struggle to thrive. But there are plenty of plants that are happy when the going gets tough, in particular herbs and edible flowers. Many native plants that were once considered weeds are now being rediscovered for their nutritional, culinary and medicinal benefits: a range of the most useful ones is covered in *The Weeder's Digest* by Gail Harland (see Resources section). Many so-called weeds are tough, grow-almost-anywhere plants and with sympathetic management, these can have much to offer the green roof gardener.

The choice of crop plants should be influenced first and foremost by the growing conditions, but another key consideration is how easy – and hence how often – it may be to access the growing space. If nipping up once or twice a day to water thirsty crops isn't a practical proposition, select easier-care crops that only need attending to every two or three days with the aid of a watering system, such as strawberries, bush or trailing tomatoes, carrots, beetroot and radishes. However, given shelter from wind and sufficient moisture, there is a good choice of vegetables that should grow well.

Best edible drought-tolerant plants

Some of these plants, for culinary or medical use, can be found in the 'herb' section of garden centres and nurseries, others under 'perennials'. All are great at growing in shallow soil and are tolerant of less-than-ideal conditions.

Viper's bugloss is a native plant that is beautiful, long-flowering and attracts masses of bees.

- Bugle. Excellent ground cover for part or full shade. Purple-leaved varieties look especially handsome.
- Calamint. Wonderfully aromatic little bushy perennial. Particularly good for sun and well-drained soil.
- Chamomile. Low-growing and spreading, bright green foliage, for sun or part shade.
- Golden marguerite. A handsome plant for full sun.
- Lady's mantle. Happy in shade or sun.
- Lungwort. Excellent shade plant.
- Marjoram and oregano. Love full sun and thrive in dry soil.
- Mint. Most types of this vigorous, spreading herb prefer part shade apart from small, prostrate Corsican mint, which likes sun.
- Nasturtium. Fast and easy from seed; best in full sun.
- Sage. Attractive, evergreen foliage; grow in sun.
- Savory. Thrives in poor, well-drained soil, in sun.

- Self-heal. Also thrives in sunny, well-drained sites.
- Soapwort. The trailing form *Saponaria ocymoides* is best for containers and roofs.
- St John's wort. Good on roofs.
- Tansy. Best in containers as the roots spread widely.
- Thyme. Carpeting or bushy: drought-tolerant, for full sun.
- Viper's bugloss. Long-flowering annual which thrives in a surprisingly small amount of soil, given its height of around 60cm (2'). Loves sun.
- Wild garlic. Excellent for shade.
- Wild strawberry. For sun or part shade, spreads rapidly by means of runners.
- Yarrow. Drought-tolerant, in sun.

Best vegetables and fruit for green roofs

- Salad crops: if there is reasonable shelter to protect soft leaves from wind, choose from a wide range including lettuce, mixed salad leaves, oriental leaves, radicchio, rocket and watercress.
- Trailing and bush tomatoes.
- Strawberries and herbs, such as parsley, which need soil that is more moisture-retentive than those tough cookies listed above.
- If the soil or growing medium can be mounded up to form smaller areas that are locally deeper, to around 20-25cm (8-10") depth, this is then suitable for growing a wider range of plants such as peppers, squashes, cucumbers and bush beans.

CHAPTER 4

Larger containers for small spaces

Using containers and raised beds to create growing areas at any level, either on the ground or on high, is a simple and low-tech way to grow veg and other productive crops, even in the smallest of spaces. If you're planning to make growing areas on a balcony, a roof garden, or indeed anywhere raised off the ground such as on a deck, similar practicalities apply here as with green roofs: in particular, checking the roof or balcony

space has sufficient load-bearing capacity; installing waterproofing where necessary; providing a water supply and drainage.

For minimal footprint coupled with maximum growth, creating raised growing spaces or stacking up plant containers in a whole variety of ways (as we saw in Chapter 2) is a fantastically space-intensive way of growing. As with living walls, you can choose whether to shell out your cash on ready-made designs, or save money and have the fun and satisfaction of building your own. Again a couple of my favourite DIY options are outlined here, but really, anything goes – so just let your imagination and ingenuity get to work.

Raised beds

A raised bed is, in effect, simply a large container. Beds can be raised on legs, which give the advantage of adding trays or pots of low-growing and shade-tolerant plants beneath, or a bed can stand directly on the ground. As well as making the most of available space, they are great for anyone with back or mobility problems as plants can be tended without having to bend down, or from a seated position if in a wheelchair. Beds made with wide tops are useful in providing a handy spot for mugs or wine glasses, as well as informal seating on which people can perch.

A wide choice of ready-made designs is available, mostly constructed using pressure-treated timber that has a long life and with a smooth rather than a sawn finish so there's no danger of splinters. Some raised beds come with additional features such as polythene covers or hoops over which to stretch horticultural fleece or netting, to protect plants from excess sun, wind, or garden pests, but these are easy to make yourself using flexible plastic water piping, horticultural fleece or netting, plus pegs or clips to secure the edges. I recommend checking the source of the timber: most garden features these days are made from Forest Stewardship Council (FSC) certified timber, which is harvested from sustainable sources.

If making your own raised bed, first make sure you can easily reach the centre of the bed without treading on and compacting the soil: better for the ground and better for the gardener, since untrodden soil won't need digging. In a balcony or roof-garden situation, where you may prefer a clean environment, line the bed structure with woven geo-textile fabric (such as weed control fabric) which allows water to drain while avoiding compost dribbling out. There must be some facility for surplus water to drain from the base; as well as drainage holes or similar, put a layer of coarse material at least 5cm (2") thick in the bottom of the bed – broken-up polystyrene packaging is ideal, being lightweight and free.

Tall containers

In this section you will find a range of containers that have a small footprint and hence are ideal for any site where space is limited, be it roof garden, patio or balcony.

Tiered planters

Tiered, ladder-like beds and frames – sometimes called 'ladder allot-ments' – are a cross between a raised bed and a living wall unit. The advantage they have over the latter is that it is not necessary to fix to a wall, with the attendant concerns over weight loading. You can make your own using wood, particularly reclaimed wood or wooden items that can be 'upcycled' into a plant stand, or there are a number of different designs on sale: some have integral planting troughs, others are

Tiered planters or ladder allotments make the most of a small ground space.

more like simple shelving on which pots and growing bags can be placed.

Permanent 'growing bags'

Tough flexible containers made from lightweight woven polypropylene are inexpensive and may be colourful and therefore good-looking too. These offer a low-cost opportunity to grow deep-rooted plants that need plenty of soil, such as squashes, new potatoes and climbing fruit

Flexible plastic containers are lightweight, inexpensive and can house a wide range of plants.

Strawberries thrive in tall pots and produce excellent harvests.

and vegetables. Some designs incorporate 'sleeves' in which to slot canes to support climbers or tall vegetables, or come complete with a supporting growing frame.

Tower pots

The concept of tower pots has been around for decades, mostly targeted at growing potatoes or strawberries, although there are now newer designs that are more slender and decorative. However, there's no rule to say that if you buy a potato barrel, you must grow nothing else apart from spuds. I favour a whole mix of superb-looking edibles in these 'tower pots': all kinds of salads with mixed leaves, the prettiest lettuce such as 'Lollo Rosso' or 'Frillice', parsley mixed with marigolds, trailing tomatoes and nasturtiums, maybe with sun-loving garlic occupying the top level or a bushy dwarf patio cucurbit variety such as a squash or a courgette.

Wise ways with tall-pot watering

The key to success with tall pots or with tower pots that have planting stations all around the sides is to create a watering channel down the centre (if it doesn't incorporate one already, of course). Otherwise, if the compost dries out a bit too much and hence shrinks a little, the subsequent waterings may run around the outside of the compost and drip out through the base without soaking the soil on the way.

At the planting stage, you'll need a section of drainpipe as tall as the container, and some gravel or small pebbles. Put the drainpipe in the middle of the container, fill it with the stones, and then plant up the whole container as usual. Gently remove the pipe, leaving the stones to make a channel from which water can percolate out. An alternative watering option is to use two plastic mineral water / drinks bottles. Remove the screw tops, cut off the bases, and make a dozen or so small holes all around the bottles. Sit one bottle on top of and inside the other, both upside down, and place them in the centre of your tower pot so the open base of the top one is at soil level. Then fill with water so it can seep out slowly, as with the gravel method.

Central core of small stones or gravel

Wedding-cake pot tier

See just how high you can grow by stacking pots of decreasing size on top of each other. Three is a good number, but if your base pot is particularly wide, you could increase the number. For stability, I recommend securing the stack by slipping several bamboo canes or metal rods through the drainage holes to link the pots when constructing and planting. While the surface growing area is limited due to the space occupied by the pot above, plants can be packed in to the planting areas as their roots can spread across all the compost – and in fact benefit from having a cooler, shaded root run.

Wire-mesh tower

Create a high-rise pot that can be planted all over to create a cylinder or rectangle mesh container filled with luscious crops. To make your own, buy steel mesh from outlets such as a builders' merchant, hardware shop or garden centre – this comes in different grades, so decide whether you want a rigid mesh to cut to shape, or a flexible one that can be bent into a cylinder. Then, simply plant as you would a hanging basket – but on a larger scale, of course.

This idea developed from the method of planting a wire-mesh hanging basket, using a lining material to retain the compost with holes that plants grow through. If you want ready-made ones, look for gabions: once only seen by roadsides to retain steep banks of rock or soil, now adapted for garden use filled with ornamental stones or with soil and plants, lined as you would a hanging basket.

CHAPTER 5

Choosing your plants

Even in a small space there is an impressive choice of edible plants that can be grown, whether in a container, clinging to a wall or up on the dizzying heights of a roof. Along with fruit and veg, add in aromatic and attractive-looking herbs along with beautiful edible flowers, to create stunning plant combinations that look as good as they taste.

Planning what to grow

When growing space is limited – very limited, if your growing area is restricted to living wall containers or a roof garden, for example, there are some hard choices to be made. Space-hungry crops such as main-crop potatoes, brassicas and onions are out to start with, apart from in the rare case of an exceptionally large green roof, that is. Hence it's rarely possible to grow everything that catches your eye or tickles your taste buds. A good place to start is with the crops you like – which isn't as daft as it sounds, because lots of people grow vegetables such as radishes because they are dead easy to raise, but then end up never eating them! Always growing plants that suit your site is another top tip, otherwise you'll be sowing the seeds of disappointment. Do read through the growing advice in Chapter 1, both in terms of siting your plants and the regular watering and feeding that is vital to success when growing in limited spaces.

Consider not just your priorities and preferences, but also focus on those crops that taste far better when picked and eaten straight away. Good examples are the many different leafy salads that quickly wilt and lose their crisp texture; ripe strawberries and tomatoes that quickly become 'squishy' (and eaten when still warm from the sun makes for a magnificent taste experience); plus you also have the opportunity to grow many less common food plants that you may not find so readily in your local shops. Or you may like to experiment with unusual and exotic crops too: not many can be covered here for obvious reasons of space, but books such as Martin Crawford's *Perennial Vegetables* (see Resources section) showcases a wealth of fascinating plants.

If you're new to gardening, start small and easy, with simple and quick-maturing plants such as salads, bush or climbing beans, courgettes,

Guide to plant types

- Hardy annual. Completes its life cycle in one growing season. Tolerant of frost and often seeds itself, so you may well have flowers year after year with no extra input required.
- Half-hardy/frost-tender annual. Completes its life cycle in one growing season but doesn't tolerate frost.
- Biennial. Plants grow from seed the first year, flower the second, then usually die off. However, again they may well self-seed.
- Perennial. Lasts for many years: dies back in winter and regrows in spring.
- Tender perennial. Won't survive frost outside but can be kept for more than one season if brought under cover to a frost-free place.

herbs and edible flowers, working up to a wider range of crops once you have a feel for the best way to garden in your own small or vertical space.

Choosing the best varieties

If anything, too much choice is the problem these days. We have a magnificent range of plants to choose from, so it makes sense to pick out those that perform best, producing the heaviest, most reliable and tastiest crops.

Varieties that have been awarded the coveted Award of Garden Merit (AGM) are well worth choosing as they have been the subject of extensive trials by the Royal Horticultural Society (RHS) and have been judged to perform well in garden conditions. Not all vegetables and fruit have been trialled, though, so don't let this put you off choosing varieties that don't carry an award.

'Heirloom' or 'heritage' are terms that you may well come across too. These refer to older varieties that have been grown for decades, full of flavour and many with wonderful or unusual looks too.

Another point to consider is that there is an increasing range of varieties bred for good natural resistance to certain diseases and even to common pests. Growing without harmful chemicals is by far the best approach to food plants, so it's definitely good to seek out resistant ones: many of these are my chosen varieties in the plant directory, in Part 2 of this book.

Seed versus plants?

Once you're close to deciding what to grow, the next decision with vegetables and quite a few herbs and flowers is whether to grow from seed or to buy plants. Of course the decision must be at least partly influenced by available space: if your growing area is very small or in a high-profile spot on a wall, you're likely to want to maximise your harvest as well as creating instant good looks by putting in ready-grown plants. If you go for this option, decide whether to go for larger and more costly pot-grown plants or whether to buy 'baby' plants (usually referred to as 'plugs'). All these choices have their pros and cons, but these are the key points to weigh up:

- Seed: cheapest, and gives the widest choice of varieties, including unusual and heirloom ones. Some plants are easy and quick to grow from seed, but others are more temperamental. Note that frost-tender types need to be grown under cover until all danger of frost is past.
- Plug plants: a good halfway house and cheaper than pot-grown plants. Plugs of tender plants can be potted into small pots and grown on windowsills or similar until the weather is warm enough

Many salad plants are quick and easy to grow from seed. Make regular sowings into modular trays and you'll always have fresh stock for planting your containers.

for them to go outside. Gives the satisfaction of 'growing your own' without the uncertainty of growing from seed. However, there's much less choice of varieties than if you are growing from seed.

- 'Ready to plant' pot-grown plants: easiest and quickest, but also dearest. Most limited in terms of available varieties.

Plug or pot-grown plants usually offer good value, but it's worth being aware that this isn't always the case. Vegetables that grow very readily from seed – lettuce, many leafy salads, courgettes and oriental vegetables, for example – are poor value for money to buy as plants. On the other hand, tomatoes, cucumbers, peppers and aubergines are excellent value plants because the seed itself is not cheap, may not germinate

Grafted plants

These could be described as 'turbo-charged' veg: fairly new on the gardening scene and well worth considering. Tomatoes, cucumbers, aubergines and peppers are grafted on to a more vigorous root system, and although dearer to buy, they grow more strongly than seed-raised plants and produce a bigger harvest. They have much better resistance to soil-borne diseases too. Grafted vegetables can be ordered by mail for delivery during spring.

readily without a heated propagator, plus plants need to be grown indoors in the warm for a number of weeks. So if you only want a few plants – two or three tomatoes, for example – it's better to buy plug or pot plants.

Avoiding problems

Much of the secret of successful growing lies in simple and effective plant care: choosing plants to suit the situation, planting in a good growing medium, planting at the right time, paying attention to regular watering and feeding. See Chapter 1 for more details.

Prevention rather than cure is always the best approach with plants. This goes for pests and diseases as well as physical problems associated with cultivation. Certain problems are specific to a certain group of plants, so if you are growing in soil such as in a raised bed or on a roof, make sure you rotate susceptible crops such as tomatoes by growing them in different spots over subsequent years. In containers, it's wise to change the compost between crops and thoroughly clean the containers while empty. In small spaces it is tempting to cram in plants, but take care not to plant so closely that there's no air movement around the leaves: 'stagnant' air is a fertile breeding ground for diseases such as mildew and grey mould.

Troubleshooting

Sadly you're not the only one likely to want to get your teeth into your crops: there are plenty of creatures out there wanting to do the same thing, not to mention diseases and physical problems too. If a plant looks sickly or the growth is showing obvious signs of poor health, first give it a thorough once-over. Too dry, too wet, too hot or too cold should always be the first four points to check, particularly on walls or roofs where conditions can be extreme and localised waterlogging of containers may occur.

Tender stems and seedlings are a gourmet treat for slugs and snails, pests that thrive in damp conditions. Prevention is always best, for a hungry slug can devour a row of seedlings overnight. Use environmentally friendly methods as much as possible, either bait or barrier methods. Every gardener develops his or her favourite methods.

If leaves or fruits are nibbled, find the culprit before taking action. Most pests operate under cover of darkness so inspect plants by torchlight and you stand a very good chance of finding the cause of the problem. While slugs and snails are likely culprits, the damage could be due to other common pests such as caterpillars or vine weevils. Remember that while plants thrive in the sheltered microclimate created by a wall or building, pests thrive as well!

If fruits or leaves become diseased, picking off and binning (not composting) infected material should be done as soon as possible, to limit the source and potential spread. If the disease is caused by localised growing conditions – such as powdery mildew, which occurs when conditions are too dry, or grey mould, which thrives in a cold, humid atmosphere – try to tackle the cause straight away.

Harvesting

Encouragement to harvest crops regularly is rarely necessary, though it's worth highlighting this point for times when people are away – on holiday, for example. Vegetables that produce fruits or pods should be picked a couple of times a week or plants can think that they have accomplished their aim in life (as in to fruit and set seed) and then won't bother producing more. This applies to beans, peas and courgettes in particular. Soft fruits such as raspberries and strawberries that are left on the plant when over-ripe will go mouldy, infecting other unripe fruit nearby. If you're away, ask a neighbour and friend to keep an eye on your plants and to harvest produce – you're likely to have plenty of keen volunteers! If your plants are at all tricky to access, though, make sure visitors are fully aware of potential hazards such as climbing up or standing on stepladders to harvest crops on high.

PART 2

PLANT
DIRECTORY

KEY

Growth habit: bush   climber   tall plant   trailing plant

Aspect: ☼ sun ◑ partial shade ● shade

CHAPTER 6

Vegetables

From leaves and pods to fruits and roots: the range of vegetables that can be grown on walls and fences, in containers and on roofs is tremendous and varied. In this chapter are my favourite top performers for all kinds of small spaces, whether in containers or trained up a wall, fence or vertical framework. Nowadays plant breeders are working hard to produce vegetables and fruit that perform well in a limited space, bred not just for a good harvest but for good looks as well, so do keep a lookout for new and improved varieties.

Aubergines

Height: up to 75cm (2'6")
Minimum soil depth: 20cm (8")

Frost-tender tall or bushy plants produce rounded or egg-shaped fruits – usually black or purple, but also pale or mottled. Aubergines can crop well outside if the right varieties are chosen and they have a warm, sheltered site, so against a wall – either at ground level or on a sheltered balcony, for example – is an ideal spot. Grafted aubergines are most expensive though they do perform better in poor weather conditions. Sow seed in late winter to early spring and grow on to plant out in early summer, or buy ready-grown or grafted plants to put in straight away.

Varieties

'Scorpio': available as grafted plants. 'Bonica' AGM is a taller variety to 75cm (2'6"); 'Amethyst', 'Emerald Isle', 'Fairy Tale' AGM, 'Jackpot' and 'Pot Black' are compact; 'Listada de Gandia' has attractively streaked white-and-purple fruits, while 'Ping Tung Long' (worth having for the name alone) has elongated fruits.

Beans, climbing

Height: up to 1.8m (6')
Minimum soil depth: 30cm (1')

More productive than bush beans due to obvious reasons of larger size, runner, borlotti and climbing French beans are productive, pretty, easy to grow and give excellent crops over a long period. Their tall growth does need a greater depth of soil than bush beans: either in containers or in the ground – and a wall, fence or framework on which to grow. Runners produce larger pods and perform better in cooler conditions, while French beans have long, slender, finer-textured pods and prefer warmer summers. Both are frost tender: sow/plant as for dwarf beans (see below).

Varieties

Borlotti: 'Lingua di Fuoco' (Tongue of Fire) has pods brilliantly streaked with red.

French beans: 'Blauhilde' and 'Violet Podded' are purple; 'Cobra' AGM, 'Hunter' AGM and 'Isabel' bear heavy crops of green pods; 'Goldfield' AGM and 'Golden Gate' are yellow.

Runner beans: Varieties include 'Celebration' AGM, 'Painted Lady', 'Streamline', 'White Apollo' AGM and 'White Emergo' AGM. 'Moonlight' is a cross between a French and runner bean and is self-pollinating.

Beans, dwarf

Height: up to 30cm (1')
Minimum soil depth: 15cm (6")

Neat and low-growing, little bush beans can produce an excellent summer or autumn harvest of slender and delicious pods over a number of weeks: most often green, but there are yellow and purple-podded types that look especially ornamental. Although frost tender, beans are quick and easy to grow from seed, so it is worth starting off a few pots on a windowsill. Start sowing under cover in small, deep pots in early to mid-spring to plant out after the frosts have passed; sow outdoors from mid-spring through summer.

Beans do best in rich, moisture-retentive soil and in a sheltered spot: these compact varieties can be grown in any upright container or in any site that offers a sufficient depth of soil.

Varieties

Bush runner beans: 'Hestia', 'Pickwick'.

French beans: Green-podded good croppers include 'Delinel' AGM, 'Laguna', 'Montana', 'Nomad' AGM and 'Primavera'. Yellow-podded varieties include 'Concador', 'Golden Teepee' and 'Sonesta' AGM. Purple-podded ones include 'Amethyst' and 'Purple Teepee'.

The bushy runner bean 'Hestia' is ideal for tubs.

Beetroot

Height: up to 15cm (6")
Minimum soil depth: 10-15cm (4-6")

Grown mainly for their roots but also for attractive leaves which are a great addition to salads when young, beetroot is a handsome plant to grow. In a small growing area, the roots are best harvested when young as delicious little 'baby beet'. Beetroot is easy and quick to grow – almost anywhere if you intend to grow baby beets, but in containers or on roofs with a minimum of 15cm (6") soil depth to achieve larger roots. Although hardy, beetroot seed doesn't germinate when temperatures are below 7°C (45°F). For baby beet, the large seeds can be sown in small clusters of two to four seeds. Sow from mid-spring to autumn – the latest sowing will overwinter to give a spring crop.

Varieties

Those particularly suited to being grown as baby beet include 'Pablo' AGM, 'Solo', 'Solist' and 'Wodan'.

Carrots

Height: up to 15cm (6")
Minimum soil depth: 15cm (6")

Newer varieties with round or short roots make carrots a recent entry in the choice of small-space crops: traditional long-rooted types need deep soil, but these varieties that have shorter roots thrive in any site that offers around 15cm (6") depth of soil, so will grow well in most containers and roof areas. Carrots are prone to a troublesome pest, carrot root fly, but because it can fly no higher than around 45cm (1'6") from the ground, you can avoid the problem by growing crops up high in wall containers or window boxes. Carrots are hardy and can be sown outside from spring to late summer.

Round-rooted varieties

'Caracas', 'Paris Market', 'Parmex', 'Rondo', 'Royal Chantenay 3'.

Cucumbers

Height: up to 1.8m (6')
Minimum soil depth: 25cm (10")

To produce a good cucumber crop you need a sheltered site with a good growing medium and lots of water. They thrive in large containers (minimum size 10 litres /17½ pints), in growing bags or in the ground: anywhere the soil is deep and good quality and where the tall growth can be supported, such as a wall, fence or framework. However, the type of outdoor variety known as 'ridge cucumber', such as 'Marketmore', can be allowed to trail without support: here the main shoot should be pinched at five or six leaves to encourage branching.

Cucumbers are frost tender so, if growing from seed, sow in small pots indoors from early to late spring and grow on a sunny windowsill or in a heated greenhouse. Take care not to overwater and, once the first true leaves are fully formed, pot on into 13cm (5") pots. Alternatively, buy ready-grown plants in spring and early summer. Plant out once all danger of frost is past. When planting, mound up the soil and plant on that so water can drain away from the neck of the plant, which is vulnerable to rotting.

Tie in shoots regularly and pinch out the growing tip once the plant reaches the top of its support.

Varieties

Cucumbers are available as both outdoor or indoor varieties, although some aren't fussy and happily grow in either site. To grow under cover in a greenhouse, porch, conservatory or similar, good varieties include 'Carmen' AGM, 'Telepathy' and 'Tiffany' AGM, which bear heavy crops of large fruits.

The cucumber 'Telepathy' produces long fruits.

For outside: 'Crystal Apple' is an unusual round-fruited variety, 'Marketmore' AGM is a reliable old favourite bearing slightly spiny dark green fruits, while

'Masterpiece' AGM produces large fruits. 'Zeina' AGM produces mini-cucumbers.

Lettuce

Height: 10cm (4")
Minimum soil depth: 10-15cm (4-6")

An excellent crop for any type of container and on roofs sheltered from wind, lettuce is quick and easy to grow from seed and reliable for almost all year round harvest if you choose a range of varieties. First decide whether you want to harvest whole heads of lettuce at one go or whether you want to have long-lasting plants to pick a few leaves at a time (cut-and-come-again crops) and then venture into the wealth of varieties available. If you want to grow winter lettuce, choose a variety specifically bred for that time of year. Seed can be sown direct where plants are to grow, from late winter onwards, or in small pots/modular trays for transplanting.

Varieties

Butterhead: These are the round-headed type with soft leaves. Reliable varieties with good flavour include 'Clarion' AGM, 'Tom Thumb' and 'Verpia'. Butterheads grow well in cold weather, so are good for winter crops, especially 'All The Year Round', 'Meraviglia d'Inverno' and 'Valdor'.
Cos: These have crisp, pointed heads. 'Little Gem' AGM and 'Little Gem Pearl' are compact while 'Lobjoit's Green Cos' AGM is much larger. 'Winter Gem' and 'Winter Density' are bred for the colder months.
Iceberg: 'Barcelona', 'Dublin', 'Webb's Wonderful'.
Loose-leaf: These are popular for long-lasting good looks. Many varieties, including 'Ashbrook', 'Bionda Ricciolina', 'Lingua di Canarino', 'Lollo Bionda', 'Lollo Rossa' AGM, 'Mazur' and 'Navara'.

Oriental leaves

Height: 8-30cm (3¼-12")
Minimum soil depth: 10-15cm (4-6")

This name refers to a number of different leafy crops, most of which are extremely easy to grow. In small containers they can be grown as cut-and-come-again crops, in as little as 10-15cm (4-6") of soil. If larger leaves are required, grow in 15-23cm (6-9") of soil. If harvested when larger, the flavour will be stronger. Oriental greens should be sown no earlier than late spring and up to midsummer to harvest the same year, or in late summer to early autumn to overwinter in a sheltered spot, where they also provide a harvest over winter.

Types/varieties

Mibuna: This produces long, slender, ribbed, dark green leaves.
Mizuna: The long green leaves are deeply divided and look attractive either grown alone or as an edging to large containers.
Pak choi: These rounded leaves are usually green. If growing for larger leaves, the variety 'Canton Dwarf' is best for small spaces. For the best looks, grow 'Rubin', which has purple leaves.
Red mustard: Has rounded green leaves, attractively flushed with red.
Tatsoi: A rosette-forming plant with rounded, green, blistered leaves.

Peas

Height: up to 1.8m (6')
Minimum soil depth: 23cm (9")

The best small-space type are mangetout varieties, which are hardy and easy to grow in deep containers, climb on any support to around head height, and not only bear a good crop over a long period but also have attractive flowers. Traditional 'podded' peas take up rather too much space in terms of the crop produced. Sow seeds direct where they are to grow, from mid-spring to early summer. Ensure plants don't go short of moisture or the pods can become tough.

Varieties

'Shiraz' is most attractive, with pinky-purple flowers and purple pods (pictured on page 83).

Peppers

Height: 30-90cm (1-3')
Minimum soil depth: 15-25cm (6-10")

Brilliantly coloured fruits borne on neat, bushy plants look fantastic from mid- to late summer and often until the first frosts. Orange, red or green fruits are large and sweet (sweet peppers), or are elongated and fiery hot (chilli peppers). In order to fruit well, plants need a warm, sunny and sheltered spot and hence are ideal to grow against a sunny wall or fence or on a balcony, in any type of container. Compact varieties are excellent in smaller containers such as window boxes, hanging baskets and larger living wall units. In less-than-ideal sites, peppers like some form of protection, such as a polythene plant house outside or in a porch or on a sunny windowsill. Peppers need a long growing season: seed should be sown in late winter and grown on to plant out after all danger of frost is past, or buy plants in spring or early summer.

Varieties

Many varieties are available, including grafted plants. The following is just a selection of the more compact varieties.

Chilli peppers: 'Apache' AGM, 'Basket of Fire', 'Cayennetta', 'Chenzo', 'Cheyenne', 'Inferno', 'Prairie Fire' AGM.
Sweet peppers: 'Gourmet' AGM, 'Mini Belle', 'Mohawk' AGM, 'Orange Baby', 'Redskin' AGM.

Potatoes

Height: 30-45cm (1-1'6")
Minimum soil depth: 60cm (2')

While maincrop potatoes are far too space-hungry and 'ordinary' a crop for a limited space, young or 'new' potatoes are quite a different matter: a gourmet delight, expensive to buy and incomparable in flavour when freshly harvested. They can be readily grown in any large, deep container: 'potato barrels' are sold for this purpose, but they also grow well in deep containers, polypropylene bags, and even old compost sacks with drainage holes pierced in the base.

Buy seed potato tubers of first early varieties – the quickest and earliest to mature – and put in a light, frost-free place indoors to sprout. This process is known as 'chitting' and starts off the growing process in late winter when it's too cold to put them outside (potatoes are frost tender). In early to mid-spring – depending on how cold it is where you live – plant the tubers outside when the sprouts are a centimetre or two long. Fill the container a third full with compost and put in three tubers. Fill the next third with compost and add two more tubers (placing so they are in the 'gaps' between where the lower ones are already), then fill almost to the top. If leafy shoots appear above the surface while there is still a risk of frost, cover with more compost or protect with horticultural fleece.

Varieties

As potatoes are particularly susceptible to blight, choose a variety with good natural resistance such as 'Sarpo Una' if you live in a damp, blight-prone area. First earlies have an advantage as they are usually harvested before blight strikes in earnest. First early varieties include 'Arran Pilot', 'Casablanca', 'Epicure', 'Lady Christl' AGM, 'Rocket' and 'Swift'.

Radicchio and chicory

Height: 10-15cm (4-6')
Minimum soil depth: 10-15cm (4-6')

These decorative leafy plants are great favourites in Italy and wonderful for winter in particular, not just because they tolerate frost – unlike many vegetables – but also when the cold 'blanches' the leaves, removing the bitter taste. Some varieties turn deep red in winter, looking particularly decorative and hence useful for high-profile containers and roofs. Leaves can be harvested when small as salad leaves, or the plants left to grow larger and develop crunchy 'hearts' for winter. Sow direct where plants are to grow; sowing time varies according to variety, from mid-spring to late summer.

Varieties

'Grumolo Rosea' is one of the prettiest, with rosette-shaped heads of purple leaves. 'Palla Rossa' varieties are very cold-tolerant, withstanding temperatures down to -15°C (5°F). Mixed varieties, often sold simply by that name, combine up to a dozen different varieties that all grow at the same rate and are great to harvest for a handsome salad bowl with different-coloured leaves.

Radishes

Height: 10cm (4")
Minimum soil depth: 10cm (4")

These crisp little roots are a favourite salad ingredient and this is just about the easiest crop to grow: not for nothing is radish included in seed mixes for children. Sow this hardy plant from early spring to late summer, thin if necessary to leave a good 3cm (1⅛") between plants, and harvest in a few weeks. Keep the soil evenly moist to prevent roots becoming woody, but don't overwater as this can cause splitting.

Varieties

All radishes are suitable for containers with a minimum 10cm (4") depth of soil, with the exception of the long-rooted white 'Mooli' or Chinese radish. Good round-rooted varieties include 'Cherry Belle' AGM, 'French Breakfast 3 AGM', 'Rudi' AGM and 'Scarlet Globe' AGM.

Rocket

Height: 10cm (4")
Minimum soil depth: 10cm (4")

Fresh home-grown rocket is a real delight, with a lovely velvety texture that comes from newly picked leaves. It can bolt (run to seed) quickly if conditions are hot or dry, though this isn't necessarily a disaster, as the flowers can be used in salads. Avoid this by growing in good soil and out of the hottest sun in summer, as well as ensuring plants don't go short of water. Rocket is best sown direct where it is to grow: make regular sowings every 2-3 weeks from spring to late summer for a steady supply. Given some protection, rocket will crop during winter too.

Varieties

'Salad rocket' has the mildest flavour, is easy to grow and slow to bolt. 'Wild rocket' has a strong, peppery taste though does tend to bolt more readily. 'Voyager' is a selected form that is less likely to bolt.

Salad leaves

Height: 10cm (4")
Minimum soil depth: 10cm (4")

The term 'salad leaves' is used to describe many different mixtures of leafy plants that are harvested when young as 'cut-and-come-again' crops. These ultra-quick plants, easy to grow almost anywhere, include beet, many different lettuces, kale, mizuna, mustard, rocket and spinach. Ready to harvest in as little as 3 weeks from sowing, salad leaves can be sown in succession (every 3-4 weeks or so) starting in late winter with indoor sowings and early spring outside, through to late summer, in order to be harvested right through the year. A sheltered spot or an indoor position is necessary for winter crops, though. Salad leaves are ideal for growing in the smallest spaces.

Varieties

Many different mixes are available, often labelled according to taste, such as 'Bright & Spicy', 'Continental Salad', 'Speedy Mix' and 'Stir Fry'. Some mixes are sold according to the time of year they can be grown and harvested, such as 'Misticanza' autumn/winter mix.

Other good, small, leafy salad plants include corn salad (also known as lamb's lettuce), including the French variety 'Mache Verte de Cambrai', and winter purslane (miner's lettuce).

Spinach, leaf beet and Swiss chard

Height: 20-40cm (8-16")
Minimum soil depth: 23cm (9")

These hardy, leafy greens are all excellent in salads when young and for cooking when the leaves are older. By far and away the most attractive is Swiss chard, with colourful leaves and midribs in glowing ruby-red, orange and yellow. The leaves can be eaten as for spinach while the large, fleshy midrib can be cooked and eaten like asparagus. True spinach has excellent flavour and nutritional value, but plants do have a tendency to bolt or run to seed when conditions are less than ideal, particularly if hot or dry. Leaf beet is less temperamental in this regard and also stands well over winter. Sow from mid-spring onwards, with final sowings in late summer to early autumn to overwinter.

Varieties

Spinach: 'Amazon' AGM, 'Apollo' AGM and 'Fiorana' can be harvested either as baby leaves or as larger ones. To stand over winter, 'Crocodile' and 'Polarbear' are especially good.
Swiss chard: 'Bright Lights' AGM has stems in red, yellow and orange; 'Fantasy' and 'Rhubarb Chard' AGM have red leaves and stems.

Squashes

Height: 30-100cm (1-6')
Minimum soil depth: 30cm (1')

'Squash' is a catch-all term for a huge and diverse group of plants: courgettes, marrows, squash and pumpkins. (Courgettes, by the way, grow into marrows if left unharvested – often so quickly that it seems as if you only need turn your back for a day before they've exploded in size. But if you only want marrows, choose a variety bred for that purpose as they have thicker skins. In small spaces, do choose one of the compact marrows mentioned below, by the way, or you'll have a monster plant on your hands!) The term 'summer squash' describes varieties that are harvested during summer and early autumn to eat soon after picking, while 'winter squash' can be either eaten straight away or stored for months. Courgette flowers are also edible – raw in salads, stuffed, or dipped in batter and deep fried.

While obviously and very distinctly different, producing a spectacularly wonderful diversity of fruits in many shapes, sizes and colours, all these veg are very similar in their growing requirements. Although frost tender they are quick and easy to grow, developing rapidly from seed sown indoors around mid-spring for planting outside after the frosts. Sow the large seeds individually in small pots, on their sides to minimise risk of rot; seed can also be sown outside. All squashes are 'hungry' plants that need deep soil or containers with plenty of good compost or organic matter. Once fruits start to form, feed every 10-14 days with a liquid fertiliser high in potash. Ensure that plants never dry out, but when watering, try not to splash the leaves and the neck of the plant to minimise risk of attack by a number of diseases.

Varieties

Many varieties are available including some massively vigorous types, so choose with care to avoid your garden space becoming overwhelmed by rampant squashes! Unless, that is, you have a large area of wall, fence, trellis or pergola to cover: the beauty of trailing plants is that they can go up and over as well as along. The following varieties are all good for limited spaces.

Flowers from your vegetables

When crops send up flower shoots, known as 'bolting' or running to seed, the traditional approach was to pull up the plants and consign them to the compost heap. Now, with a more adventurous approach to cooking, a few such bolted plants are often encouraged, as the flowers can be perfect for decorations or flavouring. 'Fruiting' vegetables produce flowers before their fruits or pods, which, when plentiful, can be harvested without compromising the vegetable crop.

Rocket flowers are edible, as well as the leaves.

Here are just a few examples of edible vegetable flowers:

- Courgette, marrow, pumpkin and squash flowers can be stuffed with a savoury filling or dipped in batter and deep fried.
- Pea flowers, shoots and tendrils can all be added to salads.
- Radish blooms are a milder version of the spicy roots, great in salads.
- Rocket flowers have a similar peppery flavour to the leaves, lovely with salads or rice dishes.

Courgettes: Yellow and round-fruited types (sometimes the two combine) are available as well as traditional long-fruited types. Compact varieties especially suited to containers include 'Defender' AGM, 'Floridor' (ball-shaped golden fruits), 'Midnight', 'Sunstripe' (yellow-striped fruits) and 'Venus' AGM. 'Black Forest' and 'Black Hawk' are climbers. If harvesting edible flowers is your main objective, choose the free-flowering male variety 'Da Flore Toscana'.

Marrows: 'Bush Baby' AGM has a bushy habit and smaller fruits, 'Long Green Bush 2' is reasonably compact and suited to smaller spaces. 'Sunbeam' is attractively striped yellow and cream.

Pumpkins: Most varieties are vigorous, large growers, though with long stems that can be trained over supports. 'Summer Ball' AGM is a new dual-purpose, relatively compact variety (a spread of around 1m/3') that can be cut early as courgettes or left to develop into pumpkins.

Squashes: Butternuts are immensely popular but varieties should be selected to suit the UK climate, such as 'Cobnut' AGM, 'Harrier', 'Hawk' AGM and 'Hunter' AGM. Many other squashes have colourful and attractively shaped fruits, such as 'Blue Banana', 'Crown Prince', 'Custard White' and 'Turk's Turban', which look very ornamental and hence are excellent in small spaces. Harvest fruits before the first frost: some varieties store well when kept in a warm, dry place.

Tomatoes

Height: up to 1.5m (5') (tall varieties);
15-40cm (6-16") (bush/trailing varieties)
Minimum soil depth: 23cm (9") (tall varieties);
12-15cm (5-6") (bush/trailing varieties)

Tomatoes broadly divide in two groups: tall-growing varieties that need support, and bush/trailing varieties that don't, so simply choose a variety to suit your site. All tomatoes love growing in the warm, sheltered microclimate created by a wall or fence. Tall varieties can be grown in either containers or soil that is a minimum of 23cm (9") deep, while bush/trailing types can be grown in any containers with around 12-15cm (5-6") of soil, such as in larger modular containers on walls and in hanging baskets and window boxes. Trailing or bush types can also be grown on roofs, so long as the site is sheltered from wind.

Tomatoes can be raised from seed sown indoors in late winter, or buy ready-grown plants in late spring to early summer. Grafted plants are dearer but are well worth the extra cost.

Plant in late spring to early summer when around 15-23cm (6-9") tall, once all danger of frost has passed, allowing 45cm (1'6") between plants if planting in a trough or a growing bag. Tall varieties will need supports, ideally put in place before planting. Trailing tomatoes can be planted three to a medium-to-large hanging basket or window box.

Varieties

All the following varieties are suitable for outdoors.

Tall: Cherry tomatoes include the ever popular 'Gardeners Delight' AGM, along with 'Sungold' AGM (orange, actually). 'Ferline' has good disease resistance. 'Outdoor Girl' AGM is a good 'traditional' shaped tomato. 'Vanessa' AGM is an excellent 'vine-ripened' type. The largest fruits of all are produced by beefsteak tomatoes such as 'Brandywine' and the odd-shaped fruits of 'Costoluto Fiorentino' AGM.

Bush/trailing: These include 'Balconi Series', 'Gartenperle' ('Garden Pearl'), 'Hundreds and Thousands', 'Sweet n Neat Scarlet', 'Tornado' and 'Tumbling Tom' series. 'Losetto' has good blight resistance.

The bush tomato 'Sweet n Neat Scarlet' grows well in a pot.

Watercress

Height: 10cm (4")
Minimum soil depth: 15cm (6")

Often overlooked due to the mistaken belief that watercress needs running water in order to thrive, this vitamin-packed plant in fact grows perfectly well in any growing medium that doesn't dry out. To ensure sufficient moisture around the roots, I grow watercress in containers that I've adapted to be extra-damp: recycled plastic bottle planters (see pages 77-78) and wide plastic storage boxes with holes made just above the base, using a soldering iron. Watercress grows readily from commercially available seed, the variety 'Aqua', but I've had equally good results from a bag of supermarket watercress by rooting shoots in water and then planting in soil.

CHAPTER 7

Fruit

Harvesting your own succulent and delicious fruit is one of the greatest delights of home growing. A great many fruits can be grown in a limited space: some more easily than others, needless to say, so the ones I have selected in this section are the best for small-space growing: in containers, up supports; even on roofs in sheltered conditions. There are other varieties or shapes of fruit that, for reasons of space, can't be covered here but would still be well worth considering, particularly where there is border soil at the base of walls or fences for deep-rooted plants: trees such as apples, pears, plums or cherries trained in

cordon, fan or espalier shapes; currant and berry bushes as single-stemmed cordons. All of these require a detailed pruning regime so it is best to consult a dedicated book on the subject. Large containers can be suitable for patio fruit trees that are bred to remain small, as well as for less common climbing fruit such as Cape gooseberries, kiwi fruit, melons and hops. All the fruits listed in this section are perennial and will produce good crops for at least several years, often longer.

Blackberries and hybrid berries

Height: 1.8-2.5m (6-8')
Minimum soil depth: 30cm (1')

Easy to grow and train against a wall, fence or supporting framework, berry fruits thrive in all but the most extreme conditions and produce a wonderful harvest of fruit from midsummer to autumn. While the best crops are produced when plants are given sun for at least half the day, a good harvest can still be achieved from plants grown in shade. These plants are long-lived, so grow them in a large, deep container at least 30cm (1') deep or in the ground; plant at any time of year. Prune once harvesting has finished, removing all the stems that have borne fruit. Tie in new stems either in a fan shape, which gives easy access for harvesting and looks most decorative, or train all the new season's growth to one side and the fruiting stems to the other. From a practical and pain-free point of view of gardening in a small space, all my chosen varieties listed below are thorn-free.

Varieties

Blackberries: 'Apache', 'Cacanska Bestma', 'Himalayan Thornless', 'Loch Maree' (prettiest, with double pink flowers), 'Oregon Thornless', 'Ouchita', 'Waldo'.

Loganberries: 'LY654' AGM is a raspberry/blackberry hybrid berry.
Tayberries: 'Buckingham' is a loganberry/blackberry hybrid.

Blueberries

Height: 90-120cm (3-4')
Minimum soil depth: 30cm (1')

Blueberries have become renowned for their vitamin and antioxidant-packed fruit and are now widely sold, but often without reference to the specific growing requirements that plants need in order to thrive. Small-space gardeners can grow bushes in large containers or raised beds to produce a good crop: young bushes can start life in pots around 30cm (1') wide and high. After 2-3 years, transplant into a container such as a wooden half-barrel, around 60cm (2') across and 40cm (1'4") deep. The growing site needs to be in partial shade and sheltered from wind. Blueberries won't tolerate limey soil, so plant in ericaceous (lime-free) potting compost, mixed with 50 per cent by volume of chipped bark (maximum piece size 2cm/¾") to 'open out' the compost and create good drainage. Covering the surface of the compost with a 5cm (2") layer of chipped bark helps retain soil moisture: important as blueberries shouldn't be allowed to dry out. For watering, use stored rainwater wherever possible as tap water contains lime. Once your blueberry bush is around 3 years old, prune in mid-winter by cutting back the shoots that have borne fruit to strong young growth and remove any 'whippy' green shoots arising from the base of the bush.

Varieties

Ultimate size is important as many blueberry varieties develop into large bushes. The best small-space variety is 'Sunshine Blue': not only does it grow to around a metre high, but it is one of the few blueberries that are reliably self-pollinating so you only need one plant. While there are other blueberries that do produce some fruit if grown alone, to achieve good crops it is advisable to grow two or three different varieties. This could well take up too much room where space is limited.

Grapes

Height: 3-6m (10-20')
Minimum soil depth: 75cm (2'6")

A large expanse of warm wall or a sturdy support such as a pergola is ideal for the vigorous growth of a grape vine. Large, lobed green leaves are attractive in their own right, while bunches of developing and ripe grapes are a truly mouth-watering sight. Grapes do need favourable conditions to fruit well, though: grow outside only in milder areas of the UK and only in a sunny, sheltered spot. Being deep rooting, grapes are best grown in the ground although a raised bed would be suitable if sufficiently high. Plant at any time of year, into soil that has been deeply cultivated: avoid adding too much rich organic matter, as this will encourage lots of leafy growth at the expense of fruit production.

Train and tie in growth every week or so, or the fast-growing stems soon become tangled: grapes produce fruit on stems that are a year old and should be pruned every year after fruiting. For best results, train on what is known as a 'cordon' system. For this and other details of grape cultivation, consult a fruit reference book or a specialist grower.

Varieties

Most varieties of grape produce fruits that are suitable either for wine making or for eating as dessert grapes, though some varieties are dual-purpose. All the following varieties are suited to outdoor growing.

'Boskoop Glory' AGM is a black grape suitable for both wine and dessert. 'Brandt' is a wine type that produces small black grapes and the leaves also develop superb autumn colours. 'Himrod' bears small, seedless golden grapes for eating. 'Interlaken' is a white seedless dessert variety that produces masses of small fruits.

Raspberries

Height: 1.8m (6')
Minimum soil depth: 30cm (1')

Forming tall stems or canes, raspberries are long-lived and easy to grow. Once established, they bear heavy crops over many weeks. Broadly, raspberries divide into two groups – summer- and autumn-fruiting, though in a small space I'd opt for autumn ones every time. With selective pruning, autumn varieties can start to crop in midsummer and carry on right the way through, even until the frosts arrive. While pruning advice is to cut out all 'fruited' canes in late winter to early spring, I leave some unpruned and these start fruiting in the summer. Raspberries like a rich, deep soil and ideally prefer to be grown in the ground, but can thrive in large containers so long as they don't go short of water or feed. Plant during autumn or winter, cutting canes back to 23cm (9") immediately after planting. Buy either standard canes or 'long canes', which are more mature and will fruit in the first season after planting.

Varieties

All these are autumn fruiting (also known as 'primocane') raspberries: 'Allgold' AGM (yellow fruits), Autumn Bliss' AGM, 'Autumn Treasure', 'Joan J' AGM and 'Polka' AGM.

Strawberries

Height: up to 15cm (6")
Minimum soil depth: 10cm (4")

Strawberry plants can be fitted into any container or growing bag and almost any space, so long as the site gets sun for a good part of the day.

By choosing a range of varieties that fruit at different times, gardeners now have the opportunity to harvest fruit for up to 6 months, rather than the 6 weeks or so that we were previously limited to. Traditional summer-fruiting types are listed as 'early', 'midseason' or 'late', according to when they crop, so choosing a variety from each of these groups will give fruit for many weeks. However, you can fool plants into fruiting a bit earlier by moving pots under cover or by covering with cloches or polythene. 'Everbearing' or 'perpetual' varieties produce a lighter crop of fruit but over several months, from midsummer into autumn.

Container-grown strawberries can be planted at any time of year, though autumn is best so that plants can establish in time to crop the following summer. If ordering by mail, choose between freshly dug plants in autumn and cold-stored ones that are available in spring and early summer. This latter type will fruit 60 days after planting in their first year, then at the usual time for the variety in subsequent years. A newer option is 'misted tip' plants: pot-grown in special conditions so that they produce a good crop of fruit in their first year, in contrast to plants raised by traditional methods, which won't crop heavily until their second year.

For maximum yield, make sure plants don't go short of water and ensure correct feeding, using a general fertiliser from spring until plants flower, then switch to a high-potash fertiliser. Once fruiting has finished, cut back all the old foliage, leaving just the newly emerged young leaves. After several years, once cropping starts to decline, dig up and replace with fresh plants. Commercial strawberry plants are replaced after 2-3 years, but garden ones can go on for longer unless they become diseased. Always buy new plants from a reputable source, because strawberries are prone to virus diseases.

Strawberries have an incomparable flavour when picked and eaten straight away.

Varieties

Early (mid-June to early July): 'Christine', 'Darlisette', 'Gariguette', 'Honeoye' AGM.

Mid (late June to mid-July): 'Cambridge Favourite' AGM, 'Cambridge Late Pine', 'Elegance', 'Korona', 'Pegasus' AGM, 'Royal Sovereign', 'Sonata'.

Late (July): 'Alice' AGM, 'Fenella', 'Florence', 'Symphony' AGM.

Everbearers: 'Buddy' is a new variety said to bear heavy crops of good-sized fruit; 'Finesse' is also new and high-yielding; 'Flamenco' fruits from midsummer to late summer and autumn; 'Mara des Bois' is a cultivated form of wild strawberry with small, well-flavoured fruit. 'Mount Everest' fruits over a shorter period but forms large plants; it is often sold as a 'climbing' strawberry as the long runners can be trained up a support.

Pink flowers: Newer varieties such as 'Gasana', 'Tarpan', 'Toscana' and 'Tristan' have great looks as well as edible fruit.

CHAPTER 8

Herbs

For the perfect combination of beauty and utility, herbs have it all. Many herbs are tough and long-lived plants too, often tolerant of dry and extreme conditions which makes them absolutely invaluable for lots of places, but green roofs in particular. Lots of herbs are happy small-space plants too and thrive in living wall units and indeed most containers. Used by humans for thousands of years, any plant that has a practical use in some way – as a medicine, for cosmetic purposes or in the home

– is referred to as a herb. Certain herbs have qualities as useful 'companion plants' too (see box on page 148).

From the hundreds of marvellous herbs available, just a selection of the most popular, best-for-purpose ones are covered in detail here. Bearing in mind the need for good looks alongside utility, I have chosen the most handsome: golden marjoram instead of green, for example, and purple, golden or tricoloured sage.

Harvesting shoots of Moroccan mint to make deliciously fragrant mint tea.

Most herbs are very easy to grow: perennial ones can be bought and planted at any time of year, although the depths of winter is best avoided if possible. Annual or biennial herbs can be grown from seed sown in spring and summer – start seed indoors for frost-tender types such as basil, while hardy ones such as parsley can be sown indoors or outside – but if you only want two or three plants, buying ready-grown ones is the easiest option and is often just as cost-effective as buying seeds, compost and pots.

Basil

Height: 15-25cm (6-10")
Minimum soil depth: 15cm (6")

This classic Mediterranean herb (pictured opposite) is perfect to partner with tomatoes and for flavouring pizza and pasta. While sweet basil is the most popular and widely grown variety there are many different types such as lemon and Thai basil, while the ruffled-leaved green and purple varieties are especially good-looking. Basil is a frost-tender annual that can only be grown outside in summer and early autumn, but you can extend the season by growing it in a container in a sunny spot indoors.

Borage

Height: 45cm (1'6")
Minimum soil depth: 10cm (4")

Borage provides the ultimate decoration for summer drinks (especially Pimms) with beautiful blue flowers, while cucumber-flavoured young leaves are lovely in salads too. It thrives in small pockets of soil – in my garden it self-seeds in paving crevices – and hence is ideal for roofs as well as containers, despite not being very short in stature. Although an annual and hence lasting for only one full growing season, borage self-seeds freely if you allow the dead flowers to ripen and produce seed. If growing from scratch, sow seed in spring where plants are to grow.

Chamomile

Height: 10-15cm (4-6")
Minimum soil depth: 10cm (4")

Low-growing with a spreading habit, chamomile is pretty to look at, with its feathery, bright green and aromatic foliage, and immensely popular as a calming herbal tea. Ordinary chamomile is fine for growing as more of an ornamental plant, though the best variety for harvest is the non-flowering form 'Treneague'. This versatile perennial herb can be grown in all kinds of container as well as on roofs, as it prefers a well-drained soil.

Chervil

Height: 30cm (1')
Minimum soil depth: 15cm (6")

The fern-like leaves are one of the ingredients of *fines herbes*, useful in many dishes. This annual herb grows best in partial shade and needs moisture-retentive soil, disliking lots of sun and quickly bolting (running to seed) if too hot or dry. Chervil is ideal to grow in against a part-shaded wall or fence in all but the shallowest containers.

Chives

Height: 30cm (1')
Minimum soil depth: 10cm (4")

From neat clumps of grassy foliage rise stems topped with tuft-like purple summer flowers: both are edible. This easy perennial herb makes an excellent edging to a roof or raised bed as well as on its own. Chives do well in any type of container so long as the soil doesn't dry out. An interesting variation is garlic chives, which has broader leaves, a garlic rather than an onion flavour, and white flowers.

Chives flowers are also edible.

Companionable herbs and flowers

The term 'companion planting' describes the beneficial pairing of a particular herb with another plant: either because it deters a pest or a disease that would affect the other, or because for reasons not yet understood, the herb boosts the strength and vigour of its companion. On a broader scale, the flowers of many herbs attract beneficial insects – notably bees, which pollinate many fruits and fruiting vegetables – but also others such as hoverflies and ladybirds that eat troublesome pests such as aphids. Not only is this kind of natural pest control very beneficial, as it enables the gardener to grow crops without using harmful chemicals, but boosting biodiversity by enticing and supporting insects is an important consideration to anyone growing plants in small urban spaces where plant life is in short supply. Here are several of the most popular examples, but if you would like to know more, there are entire books written on the subject of companion planting!

Mixed mints.

- Chives or spring onions with carrots: the oniony smell masks that of the carrots and conceals their presence from troublesome carrot root fly.
- Basil grown with tomatoes is said to improve their flavour and growth.
- Mint deters ants: pennyroyal mint is best for this purpose.
- Oregano with peppers repels aphids.
- Marigolds alongside tomatoes: not only do they look very pretty but the strong smell keeps whitefly at bay.

Curry plant

Height: 30-45cm (1-1'6")
Minimum soil depth: 15cm (6")

Intensely silver leaves clothe rounded bushes, topped with flat heads of yellow flowers in early summer. This little woody shrub is, as the name suggests, strongly curry-scented: people either love it or loathe it. Like most silver-leaved plants, this shrub is drought-tolerant and hence ideal for roofs as well as containers. For the smallest containers and wall units, choose the most compact species, *Helichrysum microphyllum*. Trim two or three times during the growing season to maintain bushy growth and encourage plenty of new leaves that are brighter silver.

Fennel

Height: up to 1.5m (5')
Minimum soil depth: 15cm (6")

Tall and architectural, with stout stems clothed with finely divided leaves and topped with flat heads of yellow flowers, fennel is an easily grown perennial. It is excellent in large containers and also does well in a surprisingly small amount of soil, given its height, so is good for roofs as long as the site isn't extremely exposed so the wind doesn't topple the stems. The drawback is that it can self-seed with great enthusiasm, so remove faded flowers before seeds ripen if this is likely to be a problem. There are both green-leaved and purple-leaved forms.

Hyssop

Height: 20-30cm (8-12")
Minimum soil depth: 15cm (6")

Hyssop is a sun-loving, easily grown shrubby herb that thrives in well-drained soil. It is ideal for making a miniature hedge for edging raised beds or large containers or paths on green roofs, especially as the aromatic foliage is semi-evergreen. It forms a small woody bush, smothered with clusters of blue, bee-attracting flowers in summer.

Lavender

Height: 30-60cm (1-2')
Minimum soil depth: 15-25cm (6-10")

So familiar as to hardly need an introduction, lavender has dreamily pretty blue flowers (also available in pink and white) borne on grey-leaved bushes in summer. The name comes from the Roman 'to wash', as the leaves were used to scent bathwater. The flowers can be used to flavour cakes and desserts. This Mediterranean sun-lover delights in sunny and well-drained spots and so is an excellent small-space plant for containers against south-facing walls that can become extremely hot, as well as on roofs in full sun.

Lavender.

Lemon balm

Height: 15cm (6")
Minimum soil depth: 10cm (4")

Forming spreading clumps of deliciously aromatic leaves, lemon balm is an easily grown and adaptable perennial, thriving in all except very dry or wet conditions, or deep shade. Plants are likely to seed themselves around when happy, so are good for colonising roofs. The plain green-leaved form is most common though the gold-splashed 'Aurea' is much more decorative, and is also more compact in habit than the green-leaved form. Lemon balm does develop flowering stems which may look untidy in containers: simply trim off and keep the plant to a basal clump of foliage if a neater look is desired.

Mint

Height: 5-60cm (2-24")
Minimum soil depth: 10-20cm (4-8")

Mint offers dozens of different varieties, including apple mint and peppermint, although common spearmint is the most popular for culinary use. It does have thuggish tendencies, though, spreading rapidly by means of long stems that quest outwards just beneath the soil surface. To grow mint in company with other plants, either in any type of container or on a roof, remove the bottom from a plastic pot and sink this in the soil so the rim is just out of sight below the surface. Alternatively, just grow mint in solitary confinement in its own container.

There are two species of mint that are ground-covering in habit and which don't require this precautionary approach; both are excellent in small containers and on roofs. Pennyroyal mint (*Mentha pulegium*) is low and spreading, and the pungent leaves help repel ants. Warning: this species mustn't be consumed by pregnant women. The tiny-leaved Corsican mint (*Mentha requienii*) is the baby of the family, forming dense, creeping mats of foliage. This species prefers sun and fertile yet free-draining soil, so is a particularly good candidate for roof locations. All the aforementioned mints prefer a good, fertile soil with plenty of moisture.

To avoid mint smothering its neighbours, plant it in a bottomless pot within the container.

Oregano and marjoram

Height: 15-45cm (6-18")
Minimum soil depth: 10-15cm (4-6")

This sun-loving group includes both marjoram (*Origanum vulgare*) and oregano (*Origanum majorana*). The former is an easily grown perennial while the latter doesn't tolerate frost. Bees adore the clusters of pink flowers. Marjoram comes in an upright, bushy form and also a trailing one; the latter has golden leaves and is the most decorative and adaptable grower, perfect for wall units and window boxes, or to make a pretty edging to large containers and raised beds. *Origanum* thrives on well-drained soil and is likely to self-seed freely in a roof environment.

Parsley

Height: 20cm (8")
Minimum soil depth: 15cm (6")

This immensely popular culinary herb is very decorative too, particularly the curly-leaved form, although the flat-leaved type is good for culinary use. Parsley is best grown as an annual: although it is likely to survive a second year, the leaves can then become bitter-tasting. Ensure a regular supply by making several sowings from spring to autumn. This herb thrives almost anywhere – roofs and all kinds of containers – so long as it has a good rich soil that doesn't dry out and is grown in cooler spots out of the hottest midday sun.

Rosemary

Height: 30-90cm (1-3')
Minimum soil depth: 15cm (6")

An easily grown woody shrub that thrives in well-drained sites and in the hottest sun, rosemary is perfect for containers and roofs: decorative all year, with slender dark green leaves and smothered in small, blue, bee-attracting blooms in late spring and early summer. To trail down from containers and to cover the ground on roofs, look for the mat-forming variety 'Prostratus'; to grow against a wall the tall 'Miss Jessopp's Upright' is an excellent space-saving type, as opposed to the wider and bushier species. Rosemary does develop into quite a sizeable plant over time, so avoid planting in the smallest containers unless the intention is to move plants on to a larger home as they mature.

Sage

Height: 30-60cm (1-2')
Minimum soil depth: 15-20cm (6-8")

Another classic culinary herb, sage makes a handsome year-round display with evergreen foliage on low, woody growth. While plain green sage is most often offered for sale, the purple, golden and tricoloured forms are much more decorative. Trim regularly and you'll get better, brighter leaves too. Sage does best in well-drained soil and will grow well on a roof as well as all types of container. However, bear in mind that, like rosemary, sage is a long-lived plant and, while young small plants can be grown in containers such as wall units and hanging baskets, they will need transplanting to a larger home after a year or two.

Thyme

Height: 5-20cm (2-8")
Minimum soil depth: 10cm (4")

Forming dense little bushes or carpets of tiny and wonderfully aromatic leaves, absolutely smothered with bee-attracting blooms in summer, thyme thrives in shallow soil, sun and sharp drainage, which makes it invaluable for all types of container as well as growing directly on a roof. Many forms are available, from little bushes to prostrate carpets, in grey-, green- and gold-leaved types and with white, pink or purple flowers.

CHAPTER 9

Edible flowers

Small-space growing areas are often in prime view, such as inside the home or in a high-profile spot when entering or leaving, so mixing edible flowers in with your fruit and veg is a superb way to maximise the 'edibility' of your planting. There is a surprisingly extensive range of flowers that can be turned into a feast, and these in addition to the blooms of herbs and vegetable plants that can also be eaten. Flowers are also a fabulous way to create all kinds of pretty and truly personal dishes

with gorgeous colours and unusual flavours. Of course eating flowers is nothing new, in fact quite the opposite, for not all that long ago these natural colours and flavourings were the only option available to cooks, before artificial ones arrived on the scene. Growing your own flowers is ideal from a safety point of view too as you'll know exactly what they are, and that they're grown without harmful chemicals or pollutants.

Cornflower

Height: 45cm (1'6")
Minimum soil depth: 10cm (4")

An easily grown hardy annual, cornflower is best sown fresh each year during spring to be sure of flowers, although it may self-seed. It bears deep azure-blue blooms for up to a couple of months in summer. The native species grows to around 45cm (1'6") high and is the one I find the most attractive, but in windy situations on walls and roofs it's better to opt for a shorter, cultivated variety such as 'Blue Ball'.

Day lily

Height: up to 60cm (2')
Minimum soil depth: 15cm (6")

Day lily, or *Hemerocallis*, is a popular perennial that grows well in
larger containers, raised beds or
roofs with at least 15cm (6") depth
of soil, this plant is so called
because each bloom forms a cluster
only lasts for one day. But they are
produced in such quick succession
that a continuing display is ensured.
Just as well there are plenty, as the
flower buds make a lovely addition
to salads or fried in tempura batter.

Day lily (*Hemerocallis*).

Evening primrose

Height: 90-120cm (3-4')
Minimum soil depth: 15cm (6")

Although tall and rather rangy, this incredibly easy biennial comes
into its own on dry soils in sun, often thriving where little else grows
and so well worth growing on roofs. Sow seed direct in tricky situations: seedlings establish much better than if transplanted. Upright
stems (best staked in exposed sites) are clothed with saucer-shaped,
gleaming yellow flowers with a piercing evening perfume. Harvest
flowers when in bud.

Golden meadowsweet

Height: up to 45cm (1'6")
Minimum soil depth: 15cm (6")

This is a lovely perennial to brighten damp, gloomy spots, such as a north-facing wall, courtyard with containers or shaded roof, with clumps of cheerful golden foliage from which rise stems topped with fluffy plumes of white flowers that add flavour to wines, fruit and jams. It is cousin to the native meadowsweet, which packs ditches and hedges in early summer, though is a great deal prettier.

Nasturtium

Height: 30-180cm (1-6')
Minimum soil depth: 15cm (6")

This is a fast, easy and superb hardy annual for a brilliant summer show of oranges, reds and yellows. Nasturtiums love the drier conditions found on roofs, and are also happy in containers or, in the case of climbing varieties, scrambling up a wall by winding their leaf stems around anything within reach. Both bush and trailing/climbing varieties are available: 'Alaska' is a particularly attractive bushy type because the leaves are variegated for extra interest; the seed of most climbing

Nasturtium.

types comes in mixed colours, though it is possible to find individual shades, such as the deep velvety-red 'Empress of India'.

Pinks

Height: 10-45cm (4-18")
Minimum soil depth: 10-15cm (4-6")

Versatile pinks, or *Dianthus*, thrive in well-drained soil and make a lovely colourful addition to almost any sunny spot in any type of container or on a roof. This flower is often known by its common name because most varieties come in shades of pink, from pale candy to deep magenta (although there are reds, whites and creams too). From clumps of slender grass-like leaves rise stems topped with beautifully marked, richly clove-scented flowers. Be sure to remove the white 'heel' of the petals, which is bitter-tasting, before eating.

Pot marigold

Height: 30-45cm (1-1'6")
Minimum soil depth: 10cm (4")

This ultra-easy hardy annual (pictured on page 155) is likely to self-sow with alacrity on a green roof, so you'll enjoy the brilliant orange or yellow summer flowers year after year. Both the fresh young leaves and flowers are edible: the bright flowers are used as an economical alternative to saffron. Sow seed direct where plants are to grow, or in pots for transplanting, in autumn or spring.

Primulas: cowslip and primrose

Height: 15cm (6")
Minimum soil depth: 15cm (6")

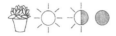

These dainty native flowers bloom early in the year – often not long after Christmas in the case of primrose (*prima rosa* means first flower), with blooms of the palest yellow. The flowers of cowslips, borne on short stems later in spring, are deep gold: both are lightly fragrant. Once common in the wild, cowslips in particular are now scarce and it's hard to believe that the blooms could once be picked in abundance to make cowslip wine. Primroses prefer some shade, thriving in those awkward shady spots against walls and on roofs, while cowslips prefer sun for at least half the day.

Sunflower

Height: 45cm-2.5m+ (1'6"-8')
Minimum soil depth: 20-30cm (8-12")

This childhood favourite with its edible seeds barely needs an introduction, except to highlight the huge range of varieties now available in colours from ivory to claret as well as traditional gold. Stocky little dwarfs such as 'Little Leo' are great on roofs, while classic tall types like 'Russian Giant' can be tied against a post, wall or fence. An easy-to-grow hardy annual.

Sunflower.

Sweet woodruff

Height: 10cm (4")
Minimum soil depth: 10cm (4")

Renowned for the scent of new-mown hay when dried, this useful hardy perennial creates carpets of fresh foliage and starry white spring flowers in the shadiest spots, so it is handy to plant on gloomy walls, in containers and on roofs. Use the flowers in salads.

Viola and violet

Height: 10cm (4")
Minimum soil depth: 10cm (4")

The dainty little blooms of many different types of violets and violas make a delightful show in winter to early spring. The blooms are often crystallised and used to decorate cakes and other sweet dishes. These little plants are perfect for the smallest of containers: wild violets grow happily in cool, shady spots, while cultivated varieties prefer some sun.

Viper's bugloss

Height: up to 60cm (2')
Minimum soil depth: 10cm (4")

An easily grown hardy annual flower, viper's bugloss is in fact so easy that it can self-seed too much, but it is a wonderful sight in summer – a blaze of bee-attracting beautiful deep blue flowers, borne on upright spikes. Tolerant of drought into the bargain, it is ideal for shallow or sun-baked roofs, or for containers in dry sites.

RESOURCES

This section includes just some of my favourite websites from the wealth of online resources available.

Inspiring case studies

www.brooklyngrangefarm.com
A New York rooftop farm covering 2 acres in the heart of the city.

www.capitalgrowth.org
London community food-growing project, including roof gardens.

www.cityfarmer.info
Inspiring examples, news and case studies from around the world.

www.theediblebusstop.org
Community project transforming tiny high-profile sites into edible gardens.

www.foodfromthesky.org.uk
The roof garden on Budgens supermarket in Crouch End, London.

www.incredible-edible-todmorden.co.uk
Inspirational local food project involving a whole Yorkshire town.

www.podponics.com
A US project growing a wealth of crops inside old shipping containers.

www.risc.org.uk/gardens/edibleroofs.php
The edible roof garden at the Reading International Solidarity Centre.

www.rooftopfarms.org
Eagle Street Rooftop Farm in New York.

www.schaduf.com
Urban micro-farming project that aims to give low-income households,
particularly in arid regions, a means of growing out of poverty.

www.urbanbees.co.uk
London-based organisation providing training and education in urban beekeeping.

Suppliers

Companies that supply and install living walls and/or green roofs

BBS Green Roofing: www.green-roofing.co.uk, 020 7622 6225
Green-roof system installers.

Biotecture: www.biotecture.uk.com, 01243 572118
Supplier/installer of 'living walls'.

Optigreen: www.optigreen.co.uk, 0845 565 0236
Specialist in green roofs.

Scotscape Landscape and Building: www.scotscape.net, 020 8254 5000
Design/installation of 'living walls'.

Ready-made living wall units and containers

Burgon and Ball: www.burgonandball.com, 0114 233 8262
Verti-Plant wall units and raised planters.

Flower Tower: www.flower-tower.co.uk
Free-standing, wall-mounted tall planter.

Garden Innovations: www.garden-innovations.co.uk, 01903 859100
Watering kits and low-tech devices.

Garden Beet: www.gardenbeet.com, 020 3397 2377
Stockist/online distributer of Easiwall, Woolly Pocket, Minigarden,
Verti-Plant.

Harrod Horticultural: www.harrodhorticultural.com, 0845 402 5300
Containers including ladder allotments.

Polanter: www.polanter.co.uk, 0845 619 7266
Cylindrical wall-mounted planters.

VegTrug: www.vegtrug.com, 01206 230025
Raised wooden planters.

VertiFlora: www.vertiflora.co.uk, 01386 882475
Supplier of Modu-wall planters.

VertiGarden: www.vertigarden.com, 01295 811833
Modular wall planters.

Hydroponics/Aquaponics

Achiltibuie Garden: www.thehydroponicum.com, 01854 622202
Hydroponic growing kits.

Aquavision: www.aquavisiononline.com, 01823 680888
Supplier of and course provider for fish and aquaponic systems.

FishPlant: www.hydrogarden.com, 024 766 5100
Suppliers of FishPlant units.

Seeds and plants

These are my favourite companies – they either offer an exceptionally good
range of seeds or supply ready-grown plants.

Chiltern Seeds: www.chilternseeds.co.uk, 01491 824675

Franchi: www.seedsofitaly.com, 0208 427 5020

Gardening Direct: www.gardeningdirect.co.uk, 01534 876 494

Suttons: www.suttons.co.uk, 0844 9222899

Thompson & Morgan: www.thompson-morgan.com, 0844 573 1818

Self-watering containers and irrigation systems

Gardena: www.gardena.com, 0844 844 4558

Greenhouse Sensation: www.greenhousesensation.co.uk, 0845 6023774

Hozelock: www.hozelock.com, 01256 812730

Irrigatia: www.irrigatia.com, 01904 202243

Sankey: www.sankeygrowyourown.co.uk, 0115 927 7335

Books

The Green Roof Manual. Edmund C. Snodgrass and Linda McIntyre. 2010, Timber Press.

Perennial Vegetables: Low-maintenance, low-impact vegetable gardening. Martin Crawford. 2012, Green Books.

Small Green Roofs: Low-tech options for homeowners. Nigel Dunnett, Dusty Gedge and John Little. 2011, Timber Press.

The Weeder's Digest: Identifying and enjoying edible weeds. Gail Harland. 2012, Green Books.

INDEX

ALSO BY GREEN BOOKS

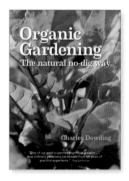

"One of our most respected vegetable growers" – Joy Larkcom

Charles Dowding has been growing organic vegetables commercially for 30 years, without digging the soil. In this new, full-colour edition of *Organic Gardening* he shares the wealth of his experience, explaining his approach to soil and plants and revealing the techniques that enable him to grow wonderfully healthy and vibrant crops. He describes how to grow a wide range of fruit and vegetables: what varieties to choose, when to sow and how to avoid pests and diseases. *240 pages*

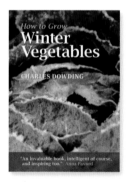

"A comprehensive, practical and inspiring guide" – Sarah Raven

This beautiful book shows how to enjoy an abundance of vegetables at the darkest time of year, as well as through the 'hungry gap' of early spring. Although not much grows in winter, a well-organised plot can be quite full. You need to plan carefully – as early as spring – for sowing and planting at the right times throughout the year. The main part of the book is a month-by-month sowing, planting and growing calendar. Other sections cover harvesting and storing your produce, and growing salad leaves through winter. *232 pages*

"This is a seminal piece of work on truly sustainable gardening, written with great spirit and soul" – Alys Fowler

Forest gardening is a novel way of growing crops, with nature doing most of the work for you. As well as familiar plants you can grow edibles such as goji berries, yams, heartnuts and bamboo shoots. This 'bible' on the subject covers design, planting and maintenance, for plots large and small, and includes a detailed directory of over 500 trees, shrubs, herbaceous perennials, root crops and climbers. *384 pages, hardback*

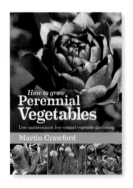

"This lovely book makes it clear that we are not just missing a trick, we are missing a feast"
– Hugh Fearnley-Whittingstall

Perennial vegetables are a joy to grow and require a lot less time and effort than annuals. They also extend the harvesting season, especially in early spring, and are often higher in mineral nutrients. This book provides comprehensive advice on all types of perennial vegetable (edibles that live longer than three years), from ground-covers and coppiced trees to bog and woodland plants. It features over 100 species in detail, and includes plenty of cooking tips. *224 pages*

"A really well organised, approachable yet thorough guide" – Mark Diacono

This clear, practical guide, for both amateur and expert, explains all you need to know in order to grow delicious fruit – from planting your trees to harvesting your produce. It covers all the common tree fruits and some more unusual ones, with recommended varieties of each. It advises on how to deal with all the pest and disease problems you may encounter, while the mysteries of pruning are illuminated with step-by-step instructions and detailed diagrams. *352 pages*

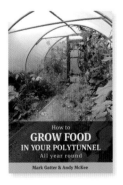

"Andy and Mark are fast becoming Britain's polytunnel gurus" – Simon McEwan

Are you using your polytunnel to its full potential? If so you'll be harvesting fresh crops all year round – sweet potatoes and late celery in November; winter radish, baby carrots and celeriac in early February; salads leaves right through the winter. *How to Grow Food in Your Polytunnel* includes a detailed crop-by-crop guide to the growing year, dedicated chapters on growing for each season, including the 'hungry gap', and a sowing and harvesting calendar to help with planning. *160 pages*

"Every serious organic gardener should have a copy" – *Organic Gardening*

Embrace the wonderful world of self-sufficiency with simple and enjoyable techniques for storing your garden produce. This invaluable guide includes an A–Z of most of the fruit and vegetables commonly grown in gardens and allotments, with recommended varieties, storage and preservation techniques and recipe suggestions. Covers everything from making your own cider and pickled gherkins to stringing onions and drying your own apple rings. *144 pages*

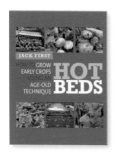

"Jack is a fount of knowledge and the expert on hot beds" – Joe Swift

The ancient method of growing vegetables in hot beds harnesses the natural process of decay to cultivate out-of-season crops. Jack First has revived and modernised this remarkable, low-cost, eco-friendly technique, and produces healthy vegetables at least two months earlier than conventionally grown crops. With just stable manure (or alternatives), a simple frame and a small space to build your bed, you too can be harvesting salads in March and potatoes in early April. *128 pages*

BOOKS

Join our mailing list:
Find out about forthcoming titles, new editions, special offers, reviews, author appearances, events, interviews, podcasts, etc.
www.greenbooks.co.uk/subscribe

How to order:
Get details of stockists and online bookstores. (Remember that you can also order direct from our website.) If you are a bookstore, find out about our distributors or contact us to discuss your particular requirements.
www.greenbooks.co.uk/order

Send us a book proposal:
If you want to write – even if you have just the kernel of an idea at present – we'd love to hear from you. We pride ourselves on supporting our authors and making the process of book-writing as satisfying and as easy as possible.
www.greenbooks.co.uk/for-authors